Take the Luck Out of Selling

Michael Brook

Trafford
PUBLISHING

Order this book online at www.trafford.com/07-0606
or email orders@trafford.com

Most Trafford titles are also available at major online book retailers.

© Copyright 2007 Michael Brook.
All rights reserved. No part of this publication may be reproduced, stored in a retrieval system, or transmitted, in any form or by any means, electronic, mechanical, photocopying, recording, or otherwise, without the written prior permission of the author.

Note for Librarians: A cataloguing record for this book is available from Library and Archives Canada at www.collectionscanada.ca/amicus/index-e.html

Printed in Victoria, BC, Canada.

ISBN: 978-1-4251-2204-1

We at Trafford believe that it is the responsibility of us all, as both individuals and corporations, to make choices that are environmentally and socially sound. You, in turn, are supporting this responsible conduct each time you purchase a Trafford book, or make use of our publishing services. To find out how you are helping, please visit www.trafford.com/responsiblepublishing.html

Our mission is to efficiently provide the world's finest, most comprehensive book publishing service, enabling every author to experience success. To find out how to publish your book, your way, and have it available worldwide, visit us online at www.trafford.com/10510

Trafford
PUBLISHING www.trafford.com

North America & international
toll-free: 1 888 232 4444 (USA & Canada)
phone: 250 383 6864 ♦ fax: 250 383 6804 ♦ email: info@trafford.com

The United Kingdom & Europe
phone: +44 (0)1865 722 113 ♦ local rate: 0845 230 9601
facsimile: +44 (0)1865 722 868 ♦ email: info.uk@trafford.com

10 9 8 7 6 5 4 3

Contents

Introduction — 7

Chapter One: Personal Success Strategies — 9

Chapter Two: Relationship Building — 47

Chapter Three: Behaviour Profiling — 75

Chapter Four: Criteria Elicitation — 105

Chapter Five: Presenting — 131

Chapter Six: Negotiations — 151

Chapter Seven: Gaining Commitment — 169

For my wife Rita for her never ending support in everything I do.

Introduction

This book is written for anyone who wants to improve their success in selling. Selling is not a gift that you are born with nor is it just down to being lucky. Selling is a process and a set of behaviours that can be learned in order to guarantee your success more often.

You may be already selling successfully and want to achieve more or you may know that there are specific areas where you want to improve. It doesn't matter if you are a professional sales person, or someone using some sales skills as just one part of what you do, there is help for you here. I am going to reveal to you the key steps that when studied, practiced and applied will change the way you sell dramatically and the results that you achieve will increase significantly. I am going to share with you the strategies and behaviours that are employed, even habituated, by some of the most successful sales professionals and entrepreneurs.

The sales technology that you will learn in this book is based upon Neuro Linguistic Programming (NLP) which is often referred to as the science of excellence. This is because it can create some amazing results for the people who apply these strategies. Whilst this is not an NLP book, it does guide and encourage people to use the relevant and powerful parts of NLP in order to achieve sales excellence.

I employ these techniques and strategies on a daily basis and I believe that they are the reason for the success of my company. I have also trained many hundreds of sales professionals over the past six years; they have succeeded by using my programme Advanced Sales Development System.

Chapter One: Personal Success Strategies

Understanding and gaining mastering of yourself is essential, before you try to understand and master your customers.

This statement sums up where we are going to begin the whole process of your development as a successful sales professional and it is the root from which all lasting change will develop. I have trained many individuals and company teams in my Advanced Sales Development System (ASDS) and I know it is highly effective. It is based on two distinct but closely related models that you will soon become familiar with. You are going to be introduced to material that may be familiar to you and to some concepts that will be quite new. All you have to do is be prepared to give them 100% commitment and be ready to try them out and apply them in your daily life. Throughout the book I will be suggesting you try some exercises to help you deepen your understanding of these concepts, so you might want to keep a notebook handy as you are reading. The key to your success will be practice and plenty of it.

Personal Success Strategies is the foundation that everything you are going to learn is built on. We start here because

I believe that in order to create a benchmark of excellence you absolutely need to understand how much your personal identity or how you see yourself affects your behaviour. If your identity is not in line with what you are trying to achieve then you end up with incongruent behaviour and that will not bring you the results you desire.

For many years now I have had a deep fascination for how individuals **choose** to think very differently. We all have a unique way of perceiving the world around us and a unique way of plotting a course through that world. The way we think, the way we talk to ourselves and of course to others, the language we use and the habits and behaviours we adopt all predetermine our ability to be successful in our chosen field. This is never more apparent than in the field of selling and influence and persuasion. These thought patterns are often unconscious, however by making them conscious through raising your awareness of what it is that you **actually** do then that puts you in a position of real choice. You are free to choose a mind set through which you can ensure your success. **Personal Success Strategies** helps you identify and then create a mind set of excellence. This mindset of excellence is what is often found in very successful sales professionals and also, interestingly, entrepreneurs and it can be attained through six **Personal Success Strategies** that I will share with you later in the chapter.

First things first

For success in sales it is vital that you understand that all successful selling is based on **three** things that you need to do and real success comes from gaining mastery of **five** concepts that you need to be able to master. Think about any sales situation you have been in and you will realise that when you have all the following three points covered you are successful. In fact I would go further and say that in sales, having these three things makes it highly unlikely that you will fail in a given situation.

1. Know what you want
2. Pay attention to what you are getting
3. Do something different and change if you are not getting what you want

Now, you may think you know exactly what those short statements mean, but let's take a closer look at them. First is 'know what you want' and I can hear you thinking, 'well that's obvious, I want to make the sale, or persuade them to my point of view'. However, what I want you to do is look at it in real detail so you have absolute clarity about what you want. Having clear outcomes and goal clarity is essential. If you don't know exactly what you want, how can you possibly work out whether you are getting it or not? How about 'Pay attention to what you are getting'? This isn't just about the ability to notice what is going on, which everyone has, but it is noticing what your communication is getting you and most importantly being in the right state to pay attention to what you are getting and we will go into that in more detail later in the chapter. Finally 'Do something different and change it if you are not getting what you want' is a statement that is really about having behavioural flexibility. It challenges the fact that many people run on autopilot most of the time and you need to be ready to change that. Autopilot is actually a very powerful state of being, and it means in general that you have less choice in your actions than you think you do. Let me give you an example of that:

Autopilot applies in personal relationships as well as business relationships, but it is in our personal relationships that the lack of behavioural flexibility is often most apparent to us. If you regularly argue about something specific with your partner then it is likely you both follow the same pattern of response. Whatever the cause, it is likely your partner responds to something you do in a particular way, which prompts you to respond in your particular way and, before you know it, you are both spiralling down the same patterns of behaviour you always do, with the argument escalating out of all proportion. What may have started out as an argument about putting out the rubbish often ends up with a list of grievances that were nothing to do with the original situation. You both responded automatically because you have been here before and you are acting on autopilot. That is what happens at home, and if you think about it, interactions with customers can follow the same frustrating patterns. Many people seem to approach their 'difficult accounts' in an insane way as they continue struggling through the same conversations time and time again without ever getting anywhere. Developing the behavioural flexibility to try something new is extremely effective.

The state of mind you are in and the state of mind your customer is in will both affect the success of a sales call.

However, knowing you are on autopilot and actually being able to do something about it are two very different things. What you will learn is how to get out of the vicious circle by knowing what to do differently, and that is where 'Take the luck out of selling...' will teach you how to generate success. You can learn how to make fine distinctions in other people's behaviour and then modify your own behaviour accordingly to build rapport and get better results. I want you to realise that this is a logical process that, once learned, can be adjusted to your style and your own situation. It is not 'one size fits all', but rather a technique that you can adapt and make it your own.

Remember that the definition of insanity is doing the same thing in the same way and expecting a different result.

What do you need to gain mastery of to ensure real success?

I said there were three things you need to do, and we have looked at those in outline, so now I imagine you want to know what the five concepts are that you need to master. These are Beliefs, State (Emotion), Energy, Awareness and Intent.

These are concepts that you have probably already come across in different contexts, but you are going to learn the secret of how to gain mastery of them to influence, persuade and sell. Once you have achieved that level of mastery you will be focused on behaving in a magical way that ensures results, so let's take a quick overview of each one.

Beliefs

What you need to notice is the effect that your belief systems have on your behaviour. It is true to say that if you set yourself positive, resourceful beliefs you can achieve almost anything, and a great illustration of that is the placebo effect. Just believing that a substance is doing you good can actually change the way your body functions. Changing your beliefs can really help when you are feeling stuck, whether that's with your job, relationship, or a customer. It enables you to try something different, and even if you have no control over the environment you're in what you can control is the way you think. One thing it is essential to believe in is **you and your ability.**

State

Because you do not operate in a vacuum, the emotional state you are in will strongly influence your customer and therefore your own success. It is essential that you are able to control your own state and then smoothly manage your customer's state as well. It can help you avoid communicating unintentional negativity as well as enabling you to put your customer in the right frame of mind to buy. We will focus on state management in detail in this chapter as it is what underpins the personal success strategies.

Energy

It is said that where your attention goes energy flows. Therefore focusing your attention on the person you are trying to influence has a very positive effect, as they will feel that energy. In the same way when someone of the opposite sex finds you interesting and gives you a lot of attention, you certainly notice it. Everyone responds to receiving positive energy from others and being able to summon that energy first in yourself and then being able to direct it towards someone else gives you an immensely powerful technique which will bring huge rewards.

Awareness

Making the effort to pay attention to your own behaviour and also noticing the effect it has on others is critical. Ignoring the impact of your communication on your customer can cause you to miss a sale or ruin a relationship faster than almost anything else. Tailoring your behaviour is part of being a successful sales professional and although we will look at awareness in more detail in Chapter 3 on Behaviour Profiling it might help to give you a practical example from a company I worked with:

Their HR Director was motivated by other people's approval and their impression of his department, and was asking what he should do about sales training and what I would recommend. My original approach with him was: 'This is what you should do, I've seen this work, you'll get loads of respect from the sales managers because it will really help them, the sales people will love it because they are getting good training…' Halfway through, he suggested we meet with the Sales Manager, who was the exact opposite—driven strongly by his own ideas of the right and wrong way to handle training. The same style of communication just would not have worked on the Sales Manager. He started off by being hostile and defensive, so I changed my approach to 'Well, there are many options, and it could be handled in a number of different ways, but ultimately it's your sales force and your product so you'll know which one you should choose.' By being aware of their different styles and attitudes I was able to get agreement and support from both of them through using behavioural flexibility to communicate with them in a way they recognised and felt comfortable with.

Intent

It is vital that once you know what you want, that you have intent behind your behaviour and communication. The most successful people act with intention behind almost everything they do and the focus and purpose that brings to their actions makes success much more certain.

So far you have discovered that success is based on knowing what you want, paying attention to what you are getting and by doing something different if you are not getting what you want. Once you have grasped those three things and added to them the mastery of the concepts of Beliefs, State, Energy, Awareness and Intent then you are ready to learn more about increasing your levels of personal sales success.

Personal strategies for sales success

Some of the following six personal strategies I am sure you already are familiar with, but please don't skip past this thinking you have nothing new to learn. We have looked at how autopilot can limit your options, and thinking you already know something is one sure way of closing down your mind to new information. Remember, minds are like parachutes, they work best when they are open! What I want you to see here is just how important the core personal strategies are for your success, and how essential it is that you really understand what they are about. We are going to look deeper into these to enable you to start increasing your Personal Success and here they are:

- The Process of Persuasion
- State Management
- Beliefs

- Communication
- Putting Yourself in Their Shoes
- Goal Clarity

The Process of Persuasion

Persuasion operates at all levels in society. Politicians want to persuade you to their point of view to get your vote, as a parent you want to persuade your teenager to get out of bed and go to school, and in your professional life your success can depend on your ability to be persuasive with clients and colleagues. There are four elements that make up the process and it's vitally import you understand how the process of persuasion works because the state you are in and your customer's state will both affect the success of a sales call. It's important to realise that the process of persuasion is not just a skill for deal closing. It's also not manipulation or deception—in fact it's the opposite. Effective persuasion is a learning and negotiating process for leading your customer to a shared solution. If you want to have a long and successful sales career then you must build it on mutually beneficial persuasion so that you and your customer are in a win-win position. Here I am going to reveal the secrets of the process of persuasion and how to apply them. These can increase your success significantly.

Establish credibility

You can establish credibility in two ways: by being an expert in your field or having a strong relationship with the customer. The simplest and easiest is by being an expert. As a Sales Professional it's important to become an expert on the product that you sell and on your marketplace, your customer's business and the competition. If you know everything there is to know you can talk with more authority, which will automatically give you credibility. It also prevents you from undermining your ability to sell confidently which can be caused by you not having a strong enough knowledge of your product or service. If you have poor credibility with your customer then you can overcome this and establish credibility by demonstrating a deep knowledge of your subject.

However if you are not an expert, don't despair because you can also build good credibility through a strong relationship. This is called the halo effect, where people with whom you have strong rapport will believe you are similar to them and will therefore assume you have a similar level of expertise.

A good example of how having credibility in a robust business relationship can turn a potential disaster into a win was given to me by one of my clients. She had a new job, a part of which involved selling disposable nappies to pharmacies via wholesalers. Her ability to build rapport meant most customers seemed forgiving of her lack of knowledge. One pharmacist reeled off the quantities he wanted of 'No.2's, No.3's and No.4's,' and she answered 'I'm sorry, I don't understand what you're ordering—I only have 'baby', 'toddler' and 'infant' listed, not numbers.' The pharmacist laughed and took her round to the display, saying 'If you're going to be selling these things then at least you should understand how we order them,' before proceeding to explain in detail. This good-humoured lesson clearly demonstrated how rapport made up for her lack of knowledge. A sales rep with poor rapport would probably not have been treated with such light heartedness and consideration.

Connect emotionally

When you connect emotionally it becomes so much easier to persuade people and to create behavioural change. We are not a logical species, in fact we usually make decisions based on how we feel about the person, situation or product; however we rationalise it to ourselves afterwards. We base our decisions to buy or change, based on a feeling that we get. An emotion is an internal state that affects us profoundly and influences how successfully we negotiate though our environment, giving us signals that we respond to. People buy from people they like and trust, so when we get a feeling, a signal if you like, that we trust this person or that we like them, or that a particular decision is the right one to make, then we can often subconsciously make the decision to act—well before our conscious mind ever gets involved in the decision making process. Even then, the conscious mind often only gets involved to rationalise why we made the decision, pandering to our need to appear logical. You can therefore think of emotions as a feedback mechanism, telling us that there is a need to act in a particular way. So, if you can connect emotionally with your customer or client and change their state positively in response to your offering or product; this can often create a subconscious signal that this is the right thing to do. So for the person that you are trying to influence this can be represented as an internal buying signal that tells them this is the right decision to make.

Whilst emotions are an internal state change they also represent themselves externally with a change in behaviour. Now for the sales professional this is a gift from above. When you have mastered your awareness you will be able to see these external changes in your client. It may be a slight smile or change in mouth shape. It may be a slight change in the colour of the neck or face. It may be a change in the direction of their eyes, from looking up to looking down or visa versa. Whatever that subconscious change in behaviour may be, these can represent buying signals to you, whether that is a signal that they have made a decision to buy, or a decision to change their mind.

Whilst you can persuade without emotional connection, depending on the product and marketplace, it usually means the other three areas of the process of persuasion must work extremely well. Relationships with no emotional connection or rapport are not very forgiving of mistakes.

Rapport acts as the bridge that helps the truly successful salesperson get over the gaps between the other persuasion elements.

It helps you cross the gaps between yourself and your customer.

Vividly reinforce your position

This is when you use words or metaphors that create mental imagery to create a solid vision in your customer's mind and it can be particularly important when selling products that are very factual, technical or scientific. Creating strong imagery can make your product stand out as more memorable and desirable. Of course products can be sold on facts alone, but vividly reinforcing by creating images in the mind of the customer makes persuasion easier and longer-lasting. It's often said that a picture is worth a thousand words, and with strong rapport, convincing someone through vivid reinforcement is easier still. You can also vividly reinforce your message by directing how your clients think. For example, when selling you the benefits of this book, if I were to say to you "Stop, and remember a time when you tried to influence someone and it didn't work as well as you would have liked. Now, think about a similar time in the future, when you will be able to influence so much better because you used some of the techniques you are learning in Take the luck out of selling…". In this example you probably stopped what you were thinking and used your **memory** to remember a time when you failed to influence. Then I brought you back to the **here and now**, then sent you to the **future** and asked you to use your **imagination** to think about a time when you will be successful.

I redirected your thinking away from past failures and towards more positive thoughts about the future, and about what you are learning here.

Framing goals on common ground

This is **not** the same as you and the customer having the same goals. It is making sure that they can see the benefit to them of what you are proposing. Most people operate selfishly and put their own interests first so it is important to communicate what they will get out of it.

Never assume the person you are talking to will automatically understand where you're coming from.

If you cannot frame goals on common ground then you are unlikely to succeed, so check in with your goals and make sure they demonstrate clear benefit to your customer.

The key to success in persuasion

Mastering the four elements of establishing credibility, connecting emotionally, vividly reinforcing your position and framing goals on common ground is crucial if you really want to be more successful more of the time and improve your ability to persuade and sell. Any one of the four elements we have looked at can help you persuade your customers more effectively. When you are able to have all four operating together they will give you the power to be successful with everyone.

State Management

Your state and how you manage it is of critical importance to your success. It has immense influence over how you act within, and perceive, your world. Whenever we are communicating with other people, we are always thinking something, feeling something and doing something, and this can be constantly changing our state. Real sales success is driven by your ability to control your emotional state and this is created by your patterns of thinking, feeling and what you do. Your internal processes (Thinking), internal state (Feeling), and external behaviour (Doing) create your overall emotional state; and this affects **how** you communicate, build relationships with people and ultimately how well you will perform.

We are always experiencing changes in our state as we

move through our experiences in life within different contexts and at different times. Unfortunately, most people believe that state is passive. States appear to be outside our ability to choose, states just happen to you, and that whatever state you are in is out of your control. We generally respond to both internal and external stimuli as if we are on auto pilot. This doesn't have to be true—but if you believe it, then it is. Maybe this example will sound familiar to you?

> *One morning you get up, fall over the cat, argue with your partner, find there's no milk for your cornflakes, your car won't start, then you get stuck in a traffic jam, someone shunts you in the car park, and by time you get to work it's 'don't mess with me today because I'm in a foul mood'.*

And many people are quite happy to continue being in that mood until something else comes along that they are not in control of and changes that state…either for better or for worse.

So what states are useful—in fact essential—for sales success? You may find some of these states a powerful ally in any sales situation: enthusiasm, confidence, passion, focus, curiosity, for example. Many sales people at sometime in their career suffer from performance anxiety. In just the same way as a performer or sports professional may rehearse or practice something until near perfection in private, but when faced with pressure, or an audience, their performance can be reduced significantly by as much as 20-30%. This can be driven by limiting beliefs about whether their goal is achievable, concerns about their ability, (whether they can reach their sales target) or worrying if a particular customer is going to give them an essential order. They may even be concerned about whether they are prepared enough and worthy of success. This anxiety is a state in itself and can also manifest itself in other un-resourceful states like frustration, anger, lack of confidence, fear, stress, and annoyance.

In reality there is no such thing as un-resourceful people, only un-resourceful states!

Well here are a few thoughts. State is active: and you can change it whenever you choose to. Being able to learn how to influence and change your state, increases your behavioural flexibility and therefore increases your chances of success significantly. Having the capability to recognise resourceful states, and being able to access these states at will, gives us more choices in how we can respond to people and the situations that we face. Imagine now, how would it be if you had a bank of resourceful states at your disposal that you could draw on at any time you needed them.

One of our most important personal success strategies, or self management skills, is the ability for us to manage our internal state and ensure that we choose states that will allow us to maintain a successful and effective sales performance. You do that by changing what you are thinking, or feeling, or doing because each one affects all the others. This means that any one thing can be the trigger, or anchor, to cause a state.

An anchor is a trigger or stimulus which takes you back to a past experience and can change your state in a positive or negative way, depending upon what that past event was. This stimulus can be internal or external and involve all your senses, or just one or two of them. Internal triggers occur in your mind when you produce a picture in your mind's eye which creates certain feelings. For example, visualising a past experience with friends or loved ones that evoke good feelings or seeing yourself receiving great accolades as a result of some success. An external anchor may be created, when you hear a piece of music that makes you feel a certain way that you associate with happiness, confidence or greatness. For many football fans hearing the opening bars of Nessun Dorma is a profound anchor which due to its association with England's football team immediately triggers recall of great English games and a sensation of pride and camaraderie.

You can use choose to use anchors to switch states so that when you are feeling in a negative or un-resourceful frame of mind you can move into a more resourceful state by triggering **positive** anchors. You will find the best way to do this for yourself, but examples might be by imagining or remembering a time when you felt really confident or listening to a piece of music that makes you feel on top of the world.

Controlling your state

When you are feeling frustrated, angry, stressed, fearful or lacking in confidence then, whatever the reason, you need to be in control of your state. Where we see this most often is in sports where great players, in any discipline, use this ability to set their state through their actions to great effect.

Think of rugby international Johnny Wilkinson—when he's setting up to kick a conversion he follows a set pattern of behaviour; which involves holding his hands in a particular way, a routine that makes him think and feel in a particular way, putting himself in the right state to kick a perfect conversion. Golfers, tennis players, all sports people have their own individual pattern and its sole purpose is to put them in the right state to achieve success.

Anchors you can use to trigger positive feeling might include visualising a holiday scene that makes you feel relaxed or focuses you on a goal of buying a house on the beach. A friend of mine creates a vivid picture of his baby girl in his mind when he feels angry or frustrated and this image gives him a sense of perspective and makes him feel calm and relaxed about things. Another has a favourite rock track he plays in the car on his way to meetings. He knows that the track makes him feel strong and confident, and he knows this because it has had this effect many times before.

You may think that you have the original poker face, and your emotions well hidden, but in reality every internal thought or feeling that you have shows somehow in your external behaviour. However, as we have seen, the good news is that your emotional state is controllable through action, feelings or thinking and you can learn to create the perfect state for you, whenever you want it.

A word of warning: If you generally try to hide how you are feeling, then believe me it's better to know and acknowledge the state you're in and try to change it than simply ignore it and try to bluff. People may not see the underlying state but they will pick up that there's something not quite right about the way you're behaving.

You cannot NOT communicate!

Try the circle of excellence

This exercise will help you create a bank of resourceful states and anchor them so that you can access them when needed. You can create this exercise physically with a piece of string, or rope, or you can do it as a visualisation exercise and imagine the circle on the ground.

1. Imagine a circle on the floor, or make one with a piece of string, see or position the circle in front of you, you are standing outside of it.

2. Now think of a challenging situation that is coming up in the future, such as an important sales call. Clearly imagine it and think about the actual client that you will be meeting and what the key messages are you want to get across to them. Having done that think about what your desired outcome is.

3. Concentrate on yourself now and consider the resources you are going to need to become successful in that situation. What state, behaviours and skills you will need. You might look at confidence, credibility, familiarity with your materials, time management, rapport and any others that seem appropriate to you.

4. Next step is to think about a time about when you actually had those resources, and were in the right state. Recall a past experience, perhaps a previous sales call that was very successful, or a time when you had great enthusiasm, credibility, and all the resources you needed. This knowledge from your past is what you need to help you get into the right state for the situation that is currently concerning you. Get back those feelings of confi-

dence and power, ready to move on to the next step.

5. Armed with these resourceful states gained from your previous experience, step into the circle and intensify that experience by reliving it, by playing it back to yourself in your mind. To do this you need to use all of your senses so that you visualise yourself clearly and re-experience as vividly as possible all the feelings, the conversations, the situation in as much detail as possible. Stay with these feelings until they peak and then anchor the positive state.

6. Step out of the circle and now go back into that experience, re-experience and get it more intensive so you then step into the circle when you reach the peak of that re-experience. You are going to repeat step five for each of the resources you think you will need for the coming situation. If you want to be focused, confident, curious you would step into the circle separately for each state. This will strengthen the resources available to you, and just notice how differently you are feeling.

7. Once you have completed the previous steps now future pace it and run it through like a film in your mind. See yourself having all the resources that you need, being successful and coming out with the result that you want.

8. Now step out of the circle.

9. Finally, it's time to test how you feel. Think about that challenging sales call and check whether there are any further resources that you need. Imagine yourself making the call successfully as if it is happening right now. Put as much detail into that image as you possibly can—now how do you feel?

This exercise is a powerful way to recreate resourceful states such as confidence, enthusiasm and curiosity whenever you need to. If you can produce these states in yourself just before going to see a customer it will be one of your most important keys to success.

Changing your customer's state of mind

You may not have thought about how **your** state of mind affects your customers, but I am sure you have realised how important **their** state of mind is to your success. The good news is that once you can control your own state, you can learn to bring about an emotional state in someone else so that you can leverage it for persuasion. Further, you will be able to control that state when you need to by having the ability to turn it on or off at will. So how are you going to do that?

The most important rule here is that **you go there first**. The simplest way you can lead people into the particular state you want is by getting into it yourself. So the first step is to explore what states you want to elicit in your customers and, just as you did previously for yourself, now write a list of the desirable states that might be useful in a sales situation such as enthusiasm, openness, and receptive curiosity. Notice whether any of them are the same ones you have listed as desirable also for you. Once you know what they are, you have the positive and clear intent of the state you wish to generate in yourself and your customer. This can be done by actively leading them, using your own state to elicit the same state in them, or through emotionally charged language, or using both methods.

Eliciting a state in your customer is often much simpler than it sounds.

If you are truly in the right state, appropriate communication will naturally lead your customer into the same state—think about how infectious enthusiasm can be! Try always to avoid negative states. Frustration is the classic—if you are frustrated with your customer because you're not getting anywhere with them, they will pick up that you're frustrated with them, and you both end up in a negative spiral. Or, if you are anxious about sales performance you will transmit desperation, and the customer will pick up on that too.

Beliefs

Real sales success and greatness come from having the right beliefs, not just from talent, skills or knowledge. Without a strong belief that you are capable of it and deserve it, all the talent in the world won't get you there. Lots of people have great talent and a lot of knowledge but they don't manage to translate it into success because they don't really believe they can do it.

Beliefs create rules in your life and we tend to live by these rules. We are not always aware of them; they may just be represented in our behaviours. These rules can empower you and lead you to success or they can be limiting and cause obstructions to your goals and make you think you are incapable of achieving them. Your beliefs have a significant effect on the way you perceive the world around you. Read the following sentence—

Opportunityisnowhere

What did you see? Did you read it as **opportunity is now here** or did you see **Opportunity is nowhere?** Here's a great illustration of that! Two shoe salesmen were sent to Africa to explore opportunities in this new territory. One salesman emailed back "I am coming home; there is no market, because no one wears shoes". The second emailed back "I will be here for sometime because no one wears shoes! Send 5 million pairs as soon as possible". Which do you think were the most resourceful set of beliefs in this context?

The lead singer of a now well known rock band was muddling along, doing very well as an amateur band, doing lots of gigs and being very popular on the local circuit. One day he decided that in order to get any further, he would need to stop thinking like an amateur and switch his behaviour to that of a real rock star. Emulating his idols, as soon as he started to think and act as if he were a rock star, the quality of his written music changed, the response to it changed, and in the space of just six months, so did everything else. Beliefs cannot replace talent, he always had that, but his beliefs led to success that probably would never have otherwise happened. He thought like a rock star and so he became one. If you start to think like a successful sales superstar, that is what you will become.

> *Henry Ford summed it up best when he said "Whether you think you can or whether you think you can't—you are right"*

We mentioned being on autopilot earlier in this chapter and beliefs demonstrate the power of the autopilot by producing conditioned responses. Just like states, your underlying beliefs and values influence thought, actions and behaviour. Your attitudes are simply the open expression of your beliefs and values. It is easy to see that positive beliefs can help you achieve your goals whilst negative or 'limiting' beliefs tend to lead to failure. Once you recognise the beliefs, values and attitudes that you currently hold, you can learn to change them for the better.

How do Beliefs actually work? Well our sense of identity and beliefs are all closely entwined. What your identity and beliefs do is formulate your conviction about things. Your convictions about things lead to your expectations in a given situation. Once your expectations are set, that tends to drive your behaviour. Ultimately, your beliefs will affect and lead your behaviour. If you want to know what someone believes, pay attention to what they do not to what they say they believe. If you believe that the product you're selling isn't going to work, or you believe that your offering isn't of value to you customer, your behaviour is going to reflect that. If you're not confident about your product or yourself, if you really don't believe that you should be there, that's going to reflect strongly in your behaviour as well.

Do you still think that your beliefs don't influence your behaviour and attitude? You will have heard of the placebo effect? There is a well known example of a group of patients with severe peptic ulcers who were told they would be given a range of 'drugs' as part of a trial. In fact, all were given the same placebo which had no medical value. They were divided into three groups with the first being told it was a revolutionary new drug that had been tried and tested and will cure your ulcer. The second group were told that it was a trial product being currently tested with some positive results and the third group were told it was a product that is probably not effective but is being tested anyway.

Guess what? Of the first group, 70% showed marked improvement. In the second group, 20% showed a marked improvement. And in the third group, there was no change. So, strongly held beliefs can have a strong physical effect just as physical behaviour has a strong effect on beliefs.

Try this

It is invaluable to know just what are the positive and negative beliefs that you hold about yourself or about what you are trying to achieve. Answering the following questions will help clarify your beliefs:

- Do you have the necessary skills to achieve your current goals?
- What are your greatest assets that will help you achieve your goals?
- What might hold you back from achieving your goals?
- Are your current goals achievable?
- Do you deserve success?
- Is the product you are selling worthy of your efforts?
- Will your customers need it, will their customers want it?
- Do you think that your company is worthy of your efforts?

Write your answers down in a list, and then realistically assess which of those beliefs are the most resourceful and useful for you in a sales situation and which are not. Then you can look at how to remove the beliefs that don't work for you and add in some that do. Your beliefs and values are basically autopilot patterns and just like states, beliefs can be changed—both in yourself and in others.

Changing your limiting beliefs

Your beliefs can change, if you change your behaviour. The key to changing your behaviour is by learning and using the powerful reframe of acting 'as if': So begin by *modelling* someone who exhibits a quality that you desire. You do that by looking closely at how they behave, how they perform, what language patterns they use, how they talk, how they present themselves. Then you emulate it as closely as possible. Next you have to believe it is *possible* for you to have that quality and then act 'as if' you have it—*convincingly.* Here's the really interesting part, when you act 'as if' then people will react to you 'as if' you have that quality and their positive feedback will help you believe you have it too. Once you act 'as if', your beliefs will start to follow and it will become second nature. Your behaviour will then flow naturally, working for you rather than against you.

It doesn't matter if it's a perception rather than the reality when you begin to act 'as if'. As far as other people are concerned, if you *act* confident and do it well...then you must *be* confident! A good example of this is public speaking. Most people actually feel quite nervous, the first time they stand in front of a group of people. It's quite normal. But, you know how people who are good at it stand; so you can adopt that same stance. You also know how they speak—confidently—so you project your voice a little more. You know you shouldn't speak too fast, so you start to speak a little bit slower... suddenly you are starting to act like a confident presenter. Then the feedback you get from people is that 'yeah, you are a confident presenter', so then you tend to expect people to respond to you in this way and this changes your conviction and thus changes your belief.

It's not for me

I know some people are not happy with acting 'as if'. Their objections usually come up as 'it isn't right to pretend to be something I am not' My response to that is to say that if by being 'true to yourself' you don't want to succeed, OK. That's a perfect definition of someone who's got stuck. If you filter out an option for changing your limiting beliefs then you must want to keep them—along with all their implications. Acting 'as if' unconvincingly won't work. You really have to believe in what you are doing because incongruent verbal and non-verbal communication reveals to other people that you are not comfortable with something. In this context you are selling yourself, an image of yourself, and if you don't believe in what you are selling, then how can you expect your customer to?

Communication

Personal success is truly about how we communicate. It's not just about **what** we say but also **how** we say it. When we want to influence others we design our communication in such a way that it uses language to capture the hearts and minds of the people we want to influence. Skilled communicators use language that demonstrates deep understanding and builds trust.

How we communicate with ourselves is also crucial. What we are thinking feeling and doing is relevant but most important is our internal dialogue and how it affects us. Lot of us are flawed by negative self talk and few of us are aware of how we describe our situation to ourselves or others profoundly affects our situation. We must become aware of our self talk or it becomes a self-fulfilling prophesy, such as 'I never get the big sales contracts'. It affects your state, which in turn affects your external communication and behaviour and how you build relationship and rapport with others.

Remember that everything you do, think or feel will communicate something about you.

Let's have a look at what might you be thinking, feeling or doing when trying to sell or influence and persuade someone.

Thinking about:

- The words you are using
- The vocabulary you might want to use
- The jargon you are using
- Grammar/level of formality
- Metaphors and similes
- The time
- The maps or diagrams you will use
- Any calculations you need to make
- How to find out/assemble knowledge
- How the interaction is affecting you

Feeling:

- Motivated towards goal or away from trouble
- Seeking internal or external feedback
- Good or bad, love or hate, frustration…
- Curious, flexible, enthusiastic…
- Own values and their alignment with values of customer

Doing:

- Hearing, touching, smelling, seeing
- Expressing self facially and with posture, skin colour, muscle tension, gestures, breathing,
- Voice tonality, pitch, speed, timbre, accent
- Moving or manipulating products, walking

It looks like a frightening amount of things that you are handling simultaneously, but the good news is **you don't have to**

consciously control all these things at once. It might seem overwhelming, however, bear in mind that you are already doing all of these things—although mostly in your subconscious. Many of the techniques in this book are designed to help you instil resourceful beliefs and habits into your subconscious; so much of your communication will naturally flow from what you learn. You will find that getting into the right state will naturally handle a number of elements (e.g. a confident state improves breathing, voice qualities and posture). The other behavioural techniques you will learn in Take the luck out of selling… will simplify the rest.

That and the fact that whatever you communicate, everyone will interpret it slightly differently. This is because we all take in and process information in different ways, based on our beliefs, associations and prior experiences. The way we process information is incredibly complex and unique to each of us. The good news is that we really don't need to know exactly what is going on in someone else's head. It is good enough to observe the effect of our communication and adapt it if it is not achieving the results we want.

As someone who wants to be a successful sales professional, your main job is to interpret people's desires—but it is very, very easy to get the wrong end of the stick. Whilst you cannot know exactly what goes on inside someone's head, you can look for key signs that will help you assess their reaction in the language they use and the effect on them of your language style and words. You need to pay attention to the language they use and any changes in their skin colour together with facial expressions, direction of gaze, posture and gestures

By the way, it's not just about body language. There was a famous research study done whose results are often quoted in books and by people generally as showing that body language is the most important element when trying to accurately read people's more hidden responses. What the original study really suggests is that when your language and nonverbal communication are incongruent, that is they don't match up, people see that and therefore stop paying as much attention to your words. The most common misconception is that this usually happens when someone is lying, but it is also just as likely to occur if they are unsure or are holding some limiting beliefs about themselves. For successful communication you need your words and body language to be congruent with each other. If your communication is not being successful, then look first at yourself not the other person.

Putting Yourself in Their Shoes

There is a well known Native American expression that says you cannot truly understand someone until you have walked a mile in their moccasins. In other words you have to really put yourself into their position and shift your perception from your own personal view of the world to how they see it in their experience. In the context of trying to understand your customer better you need to start first by asking yourself 'what do I want to achieve here and what are my strategies going to be?'. It means always going the extra mile by taking time to imagine you are them and seeing what they the customer actually want. To do that you want to think about things from their point of view, looking at the particular state they want to be in as the customer and what strategies and tactics they want to use. This kind of role reversal where you honestly try to see the world from their viewpoint in order to take a more objective view of the situation will give you a lot more insight and information. Ultimatly what you are then doing is being able to give your customer your take on something in such a way that they can see the benefit of it for them.

In order to do this effectively, you need some insight into your customer's point of view and what they might be expecting from a sales meeting.

Remember though, it's also important to have the flexibility to reset your goals accordingly, if this process highlights that you have been unrealistic in your expectations.

When communicating or negotiating with someone, there are three main ways you can look at the situation: through your own eyes, through the other person's eyes and through the eyes of an observer. These 3 viewpoints all differ, based on our expectations, beliefs, and desires. If you want to present or negotiate effectively, it's essential that you understand the other person's take on the situation. Physically putting yourself in another person's shoes is a very valuable action, and it is possible for anyone to do it. When we do this with care and thought it can often show us how the best intentions in the world may have the opposite effect on someone else. You may get quite a shock when you realise that the impact your communication and goals are having on another person might be quite different to what you intended.

Putting yourself in your customer's shoes is also an essential part of planning and preparation: something that should be done whenever you set goals for a sales call. This process is so powerful that you might find your goals change and become more realistic and achievable as a result. Here's how you do it.

Putting Yourself in Their Shoes in 4 easy steps

1. Take your own position in a real sales context and notice what is your desired outcome, and what state do you want to be in? How will you know when you are getting what you want or what evidence will there be, what strategies do you plan to use? What is your point of view? Use your imagination to describe your feelings, and what you now might want instead.

2. Move yourself quite literally into the other person's position. Use your imagination to describe your feelings, and what you now might want instead.

3. Return to your own position. See if your viewpoint has changed (or should change) from your initial position. Do you need to change your desired outcome? Or perhaps you need to change your approach?

4. Move into the third position, that of a dispassionate onlooker or witness. See how both people are thinking / behaving without emotional involvement. This is a very useful perspective for problem solving. Now go back to the first position and see what, if anything, needs to change.

BUT...

Objections may start forming in your mind on the liines of 'But I've never met the person before—how can I possibly know their point of view?' and 'What if I'm wrong when I put myself in their shoes?' In actual fact, it doesn't matter whether you are 100% right about their position or not. The fact that you have made the effort to consider the other perspective means that you will be that much closer to understanding their point of view and therefore more likely to successfully frame goals on common ground. It might be simply using your guesswork or imagination, but that's more than you had when you set your goals purely from your own perspective.

One of the greatest negotiators of modern times was Gandhi, and it was said that the reason he was so good at it was because he could put himself totally in the other person's shoes. Some people think they are good at this because they have great empathy, but it is not the same thing at all.. With this technique, you are actually shifting your perspective physically and seeing from the other person's point of view, rather than simply appreciating their viewpoint emotionally whilst remaining in your own position. That's why going back to your own position, to see how and why it has changed, after putting yourself emotionally and mentally in their shoes is so powerful.

Goal Clarity

People who achieve what they want in life act on compelling goals. Having goals and very clear objectives is a key element to success in any area. Goals are very outcome focused and they create compelling actions. Goals drive us forward, tell us what we want, and give us direction . However in order for them to be effective there needs to be clarity around knowing exactly what you want from the situation, and exactly what objectives you want to achieve.

To do this you must do some initial work that involves exploring the goal, and then from that creating a complex model in your mind as to what success will look like.

Try this exercise and it will help you see more clearly where you are in knowing exactly how you really feel about that goal. Choose your goal and write it down clearly. Now apply your goal to the questions and give each one a score with 1 being the lowest and 5 the highest. As you write down your answers, pay attention to how you feel as you score each one because there may be a message for you revealed in your response. It is the individual score that matters here, not your overall total.

My goal is ....

My goal is worthwhile	1 2 3 4 5
It is possible to achieve this goal	1 2 3 4 5
It is clear what I have to do	1 2 3 4 5
The goal is relevant to my overall mission	1 2 3 4 5
The goal is ecological, it fits in with my life	1 2 3 4 5
I have the capabilities necessary	1 2 3 4 5
I deserve to achieve this goal	1 2 3 4 5

All those answers that had low scores need your attention. What else are you going to have to do to get the capabilities you need to achieve the goal? Are there any other resources you need and is there anyone you need to help you? It will help if you use the acronym SCORE to remind you of this.

The SCORE principle

S =	**Symptoms**	What do you want to change? Is it a problem or a problem state?
C =	**Cause**	What is at the root of the problem?
O =	**Outcomes**	What do you want?

R =	**Resources**	What do you need to resolve this problem? Skills, beliefs, states, tools, people?
E =	**Effects**	What will the knock on effect be in other areas perhaps?

This same exercise works just as well for the goals you are set as for the goals you set yourself. What you must have is some clarity around your goals because without it you will lack direction. Remember, your brain loves habit and if you don't direct it, it will simply meander through life with the same old habits. A clear goal is an inbuilt compass for direction. Of course, you can still be blown off course—often by factors outside your control—but you will always find your way back.

Steps to a better goal

Let's now look at how you can make your goals more powerful through some very simple steps that will help you clarify and refine them.

First you need to state your goals positively and phrase them in a way that describes what you want and not what you do not want. ***I want to achieve my targets***, not I don't want to miss my target. ***I want to win this business***, not I don't want to lose this business. If you focus on what you don't want then that's probably what you will get. Remember when you learned to drive? You are driving between two closely parked cars…a common mistake is to stare too hard at the cars, making you more likely to hit one of them. Focusing on the gap between the cars is the most effective way to get through: just as focusing on what you do want is the best way to get it.

And remember to always write them your goals down and either keep them in a prominent place where you seem them frequently or put them in your wallet or diary to read every day. It has been said that less than 10% of sales professionals have their goals written down, but that depends perhaps on what you describe as a sales professional! It greatly helps clarity and motivation if you make the commitment of writing down your short-term work goals. Getting them onto paper gets them into your mind more strongly and once you have it written down, you have agreed it with yourself and it automatically becomes clearer and more motivational.

Next you need to be sure that you have the resources to achieve your goals Make a list of the resources that you have available to you such as tools, money, equipment . Don't forget to include the personal qualities you have that will help you achieve your goals and who else can help you. Often we do better if we involve other people to help us achieve our desired outcomes and it might surprise you to know that most successful people realise that they cannot do it alone. Now you have a clear goal and the resources to make it happen, so what's next? Well, is making it happen within your control? Can you be sure it is something you can initiate and maintain or are you waiting for someone else to do something before you can achieve your goals? If you need someone else to change their mind, or make a decision, before you can achieve your goals then you could be waiting for a long time.

Are you clear about any potential consequences, the 'knock on; effect, of achieving your goals? You do need to think about this, in the excitement of setting the goal it is all too easy to overlook what the results of achieving it might be. For instance, you might decide that you want to become the sales director of the Eurpoean operation. You achieve it only

Personal Success Strategies

to find that the long hours and travelling has affected your health, you missed your children growing up because you were away so much and your partner decides they have had enough and leaves. So, be careful what you wish for, and look clearly before you leap.

Another powerful technique is to imagine the sensory aspects of achieving that goal. Really imagine yourself having achieved it and what evidence will you have that you have got there? What will you be seeing, what will you hear, and what feelings will you have when you get there?

Setting youself a deadline is a very important factor in framing clear goals. Decide when you want to achieve it and put a realistic time scale on your plans, or you may just keep putting it off. Is it this week, this month, this year, when?

These are all highly practical steps you need to take to achieve your goals but what can make them happen even faster?

Using visualisation for clearer goals

If you want to accelerate the process of achieving your goals, and making the whole process much stronger and more effective, you will find that using visualisation makes all the difference. These are the key questions you need to ask yourself in orde to create a mental picture of what you want to achieve. Once you have done this, keep seeing the visualisation in your mind and return to it as often as you need to fully reinforce it.

1. Ask yourself what do you want to achieve?

2. Imagine clearly what success will look like.

3. Create a picture in your mind of what will be happening when you achieve it.

4. What gifts, talents and skills will help you achieve it and how will you use them?

5. Who else can help you achieve your goal—people you know now or might meet?

6. Associate some emotion with your goal—get excited about achieving it.

7. Once you have a very clear goal in mind...what's the very first thing you can do to start making it happen?

8. Do it.

Learning to set customer goals

Breaking down your overall targets into more manageable goals can make them easier. It is vital that above all you stay flexible and keep reviewing your goals. Framing goals on common ground is describing what you can do for your customers by totally shifting your perspective to see clearly what you can do for them and describing it in that context.

In this chapter we have laid the foundation for what you need to know about how to use the **Personal Success Strategies** in order to succeed. We have looked at understanding how beliefs, attitudes, values and awareness all make a difference in how you can establish credibility and connect emotionally with your customers. Now you know how to manage your own and your customer's state through thoughts, action and feelings, to frame solid goals and to really communicate with your customers because you are completely able to put yourself in their shoes.

Having done all that, now you are ready for what is the heart of all sales success, personal relationships.

Chapter Two: Relationship Building

What is the single most important thing that is involved in every transaction you are involved in? It is relationship; whether you are selling a multi million dealership or making an appointment for a haircut. How good that relationship is will colour the transaction because that is what makes those transactions enjoyable, memorable and successful. That's why we are going to focus now on relationship building. Whatever other factors are involved around price, quality, choice it is important to remember that ultimately people still buy from people and successful sales is all about building robust and long-lasting business relationships.

Relationships sell. Products do not.

A relationship built on trust is likely to be a long lasting relationship that will endure through the many phases of your career. The absolute essence of a long term selling relationship is based on trust. Building a relationship is not just about rapport—although it is an important part—there are other key elements and stages in building effective business relationships that will work at multiple levels. Building good relationships is a simple 3-step process which involves first creating positive feelings in others, then determining mutually satisfying goals and finally establishing and maintaining rapport. They do not exist in isolation but are continually cycling round supporting and feeding each other.

Step 1: Creating positive feelings in others

This is all about getting your customer into the right state and we looked at how to do that in the last chapter. It's about you making them feel good in themselves and making them feel good about you and what you are offering. What's important here is that you ensure that they associate that state of feeling good with you. If you can make people feel really good about you, then business tends to naturally come from that relationship. Have you ever been for an interview for a job that you desperately wanted and you were so focused on the outcome of 'getting the job' that you performed at less than your best, your communication was actually quite poor and as a result, you ended up not getting it? What about the opposite experience where you get an interview for a job you don't need or are not sure about? Usually, you focus more attention on making sure that the interviewer has a fantastic experience and good feeling about you, rather than on getting the job and the irony is that in that situation you often end up getting offered it anyway!

BE AWARE: Creating negative as well as positive feelings in others can occur so you need to be aware of the effect you are having. This particularly applies if you are applying selling techniques that encourages customers to form negative associations with you by creating negative states. For instance some sales professionals selling financial services tend to focus the client on the problems they may be experiencing, or could experience, in the future. They then get the client to think about the implication of these problems. This can totally undermine the concept of building a long-lasting business relationship as the client may form a negative anchor to you and your products therefore should be used with great caution.

Step 2: Determining mutually satisfying goals

What you are looking to do here is to be able to elegantly communicate what you want in such a way that the customer can clearly see the benefits for them and not necessarily the benefits for you. If you go into a relationship or a sale only understanding the situation from your own viewpoint, and you've not considered your customer at all, then you are unlikely to have identified or set goals that are mutually satisfying. Also you are not going to be communicating those goals in a way that is attractive to your customer. This frequently leads to failure that almost certainly could have been avoided with careful attention to planning.

Step 3: Establishing and maintaining rapport

This needs to be done at as many levels as possible, conceptually, physiologically and emotionally. Rapport is undoubtedly an essential part of the process, although it is only one part and not the entity. We'll come back to rapport in a short while and look at it in a lot more detail.

Having taken a brief overview of the three important elements in relationship building, we can now build on what you learned in chapter one about Personal Success Strategies, Goal Setting, State Management and Putting Yourself in Their Shoes, as they have given us the foundation for the next stage of going deeper into exactly how you put all the necessary elements in place.

1. How to create positive feelings in detail

You now know that we can all control our own state. Once you have yourself in a desired state, or a desired state that would be useful to you and to the customer, you can lead them into that same state as well, but remember you must go there first. You might want to take a look back and see what states you chose in Chapter 1 that it would be useful to have your customer in.

Once you are comfortable, and more skilled in eliciting the right state with your customer, then you can also create an anchor for them that they associate with that state. You can then use this anchor to bring out that state in them more quickly and easily the next time you need to because they will associate it with you and be more prepared to go there.

How do I set an anchor?

The most potent time to set an anchor is before your customer reaches their peak in the state. You can learn to tell which stage they are at through observation and practice and one group of people who are masters at those arts are stand up comedians. One who is particularly brilliant at setting and using anchors as part of his stand-up comedy routine is Eddie Izzard.

If one of his gags doesn't get a laugh, or fails to get a big enough laugh, he walks over to the other side of the stage and pulls an imaginary notebook and pen out of his back pocket, pretends to open it to a blank page and to note down not to use that joke again. He talks aloud whilst doing this so the audience knows exactly what he is doing and then he folds the invisible book and places it back in his pocket before returning to the other side of the stage. Usually, just going through these actions will get him a laugh anyway and throughout his routine, each time there is any kind of a problem, he will go through the same routine—walking to the other side of the stage, getting out his notebook, and writing down notes. Setting this combination of anchors works so well that within a short time he only has to start to walk to the other side of the stage for people to begin laughing.

He is setting a very positive set of anchors for the audience, but it is equally possible to set negative anchors without meaning to do so. If you show frustration or anxiety in front of your customer it might not only affect that one meeting. Do it more than once and they may start to associate these negative feelings and states with your presence! It doesn't mean your customer is now lost forever, however you will have to work that much harder to create positive feelings about you. Remember, you set an anchor by using it whilst your customer is in the state you want. It is always a good idea to test the anchor for effectiveness, so use it when the customer is in a different state to the one you want and see what their response is. If they change state and the test works, you can use the anchor whenever you want them in that state. If it doesn't work, you need to set the anchor better. Lead them back into the desired state and set the anchor again. Each time you do this, the association will become stronger.

2. Creating mutually satisfying goals

In Personal Success Strategies we saw how important goal clarity is. One of the most important steps in sales success is to Know What You Want. You did this by putting yourself in the first position (your position) and then using the goal setting strategies for defining what you want. Most people make decisions from a selfish perspective and therefore it's essential to be able to communicate what you want, and what your expectations are in terms of the benefits they will receive. You can achieve this by going to the second position (their position) and seeing it from their point of view.

Always answer their biggest question: What's in it for me?

You need to consider what your goals are in terms of the business you are in and that might mean more sales, increased profit, broadening the range of products you sell to this customer, or better customer interaction. Whatever your business, it's essential you think about what goals you have for the relationship and how that can develop. Finally, it is also important for you to consider who is involved in your achievement of this goal.

Take a moment now and, using the goal setting techniques covered in Personal Success Strategies, determine what your goals are for a given relationship in this context.

What kind of relationship do you want?

If you don't define your relationship goals as clearly as your other goals you are setting yourself up for misunderstandings and missed opportunities.

Pay close attention to the effects of communicating your goals. As you will see later it is essential to be able to calibrate what effect your communication is having so you must pay attention to what result you are getting. This helps you to recognise whether your customer really understands how they will benefit from the achievement of your goal. It's not enough just to pay attention to the effect your communication is having. If you don't seem to be getting the response you'd hoped for you must have the flexibility to do something different.

To sum it up, it's a three step process: first know what you want, then notice what you are getting, and finally be flexible enough to do something different if you are not getting what you want.

3. How to establish and maintain rapport in detail

This is an area where we will cover a lot of ground, so let me first give you a route map for where we are going. Rapport involves a number of elements and some of them you have already encountered previously. Rapport involves matching and pacing, using calibration, and using your awareness and observation of your customer's physiological responses to you, what they sound like and what words they use, specifically what sensory words they offer you. You also need to understand what your customer's values and beliefs are, though you do not necessarily have to match them if they are in conflict with your own values and beliefs. Knowing all this information about your customer will more naturally bring you to a state of intense interest in them, and that will radically affect how they respond to you.

Rapport is often the first key element of a good relationship, because it helps the process of communication between you and your customer. It can be established at many levels, in fact the more, the better. Rapport has several elements, and you probably know what you think it means for you, so let's look first at what it isn't to see if we have the same ideas.

First, do not confuse it with friendship because it is not the same thing. It is not measured by being 'friends' with your customers. You can have excellent rapport and a business relationship that serves its purpose without being best friends. It's also possible to have a great friendship with a customer without achieving your business goals. Secondly, it is not the same as trust, though rapport can help you to begin establishing it. Rapport is something that can be established very quickly, sometimes instantly, but trust is not established immediately, it takes time to build. Finally, rapport alone is not the same as a good business relationship. It may be an essential part of it, but it is not always true that the deeper the rapport the better your business performance will be. It's possible to establish such a deep rapport with your customer that you see and identify with their point of view so strongly that you end up backing away from your goals. That defies the whole point of establishing rapport in a business context. When establishing rapport it is essential you keep your intention crystal clear and your goals in sight at all times.

So what IS rapport?

Now you can begin to see more clearly what defines rapport, and in essence it is perceived similarity.

In other words, people tend to like people they perceive to be like themselves.

Relationship Building

That doesn't mean that you and your customer have to be alike, just that you are able to minimise the perceived differences between you. Now these differences may lie in many different areas, but the more levels on which you can minimise the differences, then the stronger the rapport you will create. Human nature being what it is, we tend to seek out and prefer the company of 'people like us'. This is because it makes us feel more comfortable and, in turn, we are more easily led, persuaded and influenced by similar people. This is the situation that you ideally want to be creating with your customers. It is all about minimising the perceived differences between you and your customer and you do this by matching, pacing and leading your customer's state. When you match, you identify the state your customer is in and then look for ways you can match with them. When you are pacing them you go beyond identifying and actually do it. Finally if you have checked that you are effectively pacing your customer, you should now be able to lead them into the state you would like them to be in. If you are also in that same state they will be more receptive to your communication because the accuracy of your rapport depends on how accurately you can replicate your customer's state.

This isn't rocket science—in fact all the things you do to establish rapport are just the same things that normally happen at a completely unconscious level whenever we are communicating with other people effectively. All you need to learn is how to apply them consciously so you can make that relationship work a little better or quicker, or perhaps just make it more workable than it was before.

Developing rapport

Let's start with a caution: rapport cannot be established then forgotten, it is a constant dynamic and requires constant attention. It is high maintenance so you have to be vigilant and aware of your relationship to your customer at all times. Because rapport is totally dynamic, free flowing and constantly changing you have to really pay attention and be routinely checking to see where the level of rapport is at any given moment. In other words, constant vigilance is the price you pay for good business relationships. The good news is that the more you practice building rapport, the easier it becomes. We are going to look at both non-verbal and verbal rapport and you do exactly the same things to build rapport in both cases.

Establishing rapport

As we have already seen, in order to get closer to your customer you want to be able to build rapport with them accurately, and at as many levels as possible. When you can accurately replicate your customer's state then the closer will be the rapport between you. So what's the best way to do that? This is where our route map comes into play that we looked at earlier in the chapter. The key words here are **match, pace, calibrate and lead.** First you want to identify what you can match and pace, calibrate which means observing carefully to check if it's working, and then lead them into the desired state.

Building rapport by matching and pacing

Matching is where you identify the state your customer is in, and look for ways you can match with them. You do this by observing the verbal and non-verbal signals everyone gives out and perhaps the most obvious area to look at first are the physiological, or physical signs that you pick up in any interaction. Physiological signals cover body language so you look at their posture, facial expressions, gestures, eye contact and breathing. It also includes speech, how they actually sound to you, so you would be looking at breathing, how fast or slowly they are speaking, how much energy and volume they are putting out and what is their accent, pitch and articulation. The key thing to master here is subtlety because there is a very fine balance between matching and pacing, and outright mimicking. If you are obviously mirroring, or copying, a person's gestures and they notice you doing any of these things, you can undo all the good you have achieved so try to keep the things you match as far below consciousness as possible. As a rough guide, people are more likely to notice you mirroring their posture, gestures or accent but less likely to be aware of you matching facial expressions, breathing, and eye contact.

Exercise:—have a conversation for 5 minutes with someone on any non-controversial subject and really pay attention to the other person's physiology and tonality. Look at their posture, gestures, expressions, the sound of their voice, and try to match as many of those things as you possibly can. Notice if you were pacing, matching or leading and then continue the conversation and this time try to deliberately mismatch as many things as you can. What you will probably find is that it seems almost impossible to do. That's normal, because mismatching feels rude, wrong, and it violates all your values and beliefs and most importantly what it actually does is to breakdown communication.

Physiological signals are not the only ones you will want to match, and we will be looking later in the chapter at the other elements such as values, beliefs and words.

From non-verbal rapport to linguistic rapport

If you really pay attention to what people are saying, the actual words they use, then you will notice that everyone has certain key words or phrases that they use frequently. They are 'buzz' words or personal trance words that have deep personal meaning for them, and if you play these back to them then they know that you know what they mean. You have immediately established rapport by demonstrating a deep understanding that you do comprehend and know what they are talking about. It is exactly the same if you are working with an individual or an organisation. Companies often have their own language to describe processes or events, and specialised phraseology for industries like IT and engineering. If when you first visit a new company you can show that you can speak with them in their own language you will demonstrate that you are 'someone like us' which is an excellent way to establish rapport. Key tools to enable you to achieve this are using 'parrot phrasing', not paraphrasing, and echoing back to them their own words and phrases. A reminder here not to use paraphrasing, which is part of active listening, where you restate their words in your own language. This actually breaks rapport while they try to work out what you mean as opposed to what they said.

One of the great delights of the human condition is that we all see the world in different ways. Our perception of the world, reality, events and communication is unique and tends to be rooted most strongly in one of our senses. A very powerful way to build rapport is to understand and communicate with them using their own words and sensory preferences.

How we speak, our actual choice of words, can reflect emotional associations and also reveal our preferred sensory mode. We all operate predominantly through being Visual (seeing), Auditory (hearing) or Kinaesthetic (feeling) and Unspecified. The last category (Unspecified) is used to classify words or phrases that don't fit into any sensory category.

To give you an idea of where you fit in, and show you the words to watch for in your customers, you might want to try the following exercise:

Exercise:

To see if you have a clear idea of which category they fall into, mark the following words and phrases with a V for Visual, A for Auditory, K for Kinaesthetic or U for Unspecified:

I see now	Pleasing personality
Too loud for me	Ruffled some feathers
Hot idea	Quiet please
What an oversight	Rings a bell
Bright idea	Awesome potential
Move back	Let's set our view
Chime in	Branching out

Shakes me up	Brilliant example
Pretty picture	A tender moment
Understand completely	Soft sell
Don't utter a word	Observe if you will
Lovely view	Tone it down
I hear you	That blows me away
Solid idea	Someone told me
Get the big picture	Bells & whistles
Rough day	All singing, all dancing

There are obviously some key words and phrases that are often used by each type so it's helpful to have a reference if you are not sure, or to deepen your knowledge before you meet a new customer.

Visual clues

If you think your customer is predominantly visual, these are the kinds of words they will be using:

See	Cloudy	Picture
Aim	Watch	Blind
Dark	Light	Clear
Sketch	Reflect	Zoom in
View	Dim	Image
Glow	Observe	Foggy
Portray	Pretty	Sight
Bright	Visible	Survey
Scan	Hide	Glare
Vision	Focus	Reveal
Hazy	Brilliant	Shine
Dull	Oversight	Spotless
Colour	Diagram	Draw
Show	Look	

Auditory clues

If you think your customer is predominantly auditory, these are the kinds of words they will be using:

Speak	Loud	Purr
Hear	Clatter	Call
Say	Aloud	Chant
Talk	Shrill	Noise
Yell	Verbalise	Listen
Rasp	Clang	Ring
Sing	Squawk	Voice
Babble	Debate	Scream
Whine	Utter	Sound
Tone	Shriek	Shout
Boom	Hiss	Tune
Chime	Resounding	
Snore	Tell	
Music	Discuss	
Describe	Phrase	

Kinaesthetic clues

If you think your customer is predominantly kinaesthetic, these are the kinds of words they will be using:

Feel	Push	Warm
String	Reach	Shoulder
Sharp	Connect	Grasp
Fumble	Jarring	Stick
Cool	Link	Solid
Balanced	Cram	Shape
Shocking	Tackle	Hard
Merge	Pack	Soft
Bumpy	Shuffle	Handle
Bend	Unite	Fall
Throw	Catch	Cut
Rough	Strain	Lift
Grasp	Sharp	Strain
Tension	Compress	

Take the luck *out of* selling

Unspecified clues

These are the kind of words that fit into the unspecified category:

Logical

Organise

Express

Evaluate

Feedback

Explain

Ponder

Select

Rational

Cooperate

Interact

Understand

Teach

Reward

Plan

Relate

Reiterate

Agree

Condone

Communicate

Worrisome

Decide

Hope

Remember, they can be giving off signals in more than one area so pay attention and once you have established what mode your customer is operating in, you can communicate more effectively by tuning in to their sensory preference and using words that are appropriate for them. This will help you feel more in tune with your customer's current mode, enabling them to see more easily what you are trying to communicate. This will help build rapport and make your task of influence and persuasion much easier. However, first you need to be sure that you are accurately reflecting what your customer is saying.

Parrot phrasing or echoing to establish rapport

The first and most obvious way to check this involves simply using people's words back to them. Pay attention to your customer's personal buzz or personal trance words; the phrases that they love and will always use in a particular context. These are naturally occurring linguistic anchors, and you can create rapport just by using their own words back to them and by using the same tonal qualities they are using such as pitch and pace. They may have a whole stack of deep-rooted beliefs and meanings built around each word and if you say it back to them, you know you're going to get a great response. Whatever vocabulary someone uses, you can always know one thing for sure.

THEY understand what THEY mean.

You might not understand someone else's choice of words, but you can bet that they certainly do. So, if you use their actual words back to them, that is what we call 'parrot phrase' then you can bet that they will understand you clearly. Parrot Phrasing is about dripping their words back into the conversation which has the effect that they feel really understood and heard by you. We have used the phrase **PARROT PHRASING NOT PARAPHRASING** to sum that up, however, it's not quite as easy as that. The problem with the usual approach of summarising or paraphrasing, in the context of rapport building, is that we try to reframe what the other person has said rather than using their exact words. This is what is traditionally done with the approach of active listening, where you listen to the customer, hear what they've said and reformat their sentence into your own words, so that you are paraphrasing it back to them, in a changed way. This leads to misunderstanding as much of the meaning is lost with the change of words. To prevent this happening you need to literally echo their words back to them and not paraphrase. For instance, you may say to me 'Advanced Sales Development System (ASDS) is by far and away the best sales training course I've ever seen'. I am delighted to hear that and later in the conversation I say back to you 'OK, so you think ASDS is a fantastic way of learning sales'. I have just paraphrased what I think you meant, but it may not be exactly what you intended me to understand. It is important that I then check if we do indeed mean the same thing or if I have distorted the meaning of your words. Whilst this may all happen quite quickly during a conversation, there is still a period of inertia or doubt that makes the experience less positive than parrot phrasing. Your customer is using specific phrases for a good reason, so reinforce the rapport by parroting them back.

Matching Beliefs and/or Values

Beliefs and Values are to some extent intertwined. Values are what are important to someone, and they can cover almost anything including freedom, change, flexibility, control, power and honesty. Beliefs are more deep rooted and can include spirituality, political attitudes, codes of conduct and standards of personal behaviour. These may be hard to match for many people and it's not advisable to try unless you genuinely share that belief on a deep level. It is much more important to simply demonstrate an understanding of them.

There is a natural tendency in all of us to seek common ground with each other. This may exist in our values, our backgrounds, our actions, or our interests. Your aim when you are matching in this area is to focus on minimising the perceived differences between you, but it does not mean pretending to be the same as your customer. It is most naturally achieved by focusing on one small part of a belief or value rather than trying to reproduce the whole area. One of the oldest techniques that has been applied in this area is where the sales person searches for 'common ground' with their customer in the area of hobbies, interests, or sports. Provided you handle this honestly, it can be very effective, BUT because it tends to be one of the easiest areas to identify there is a danger of overusing it so be on the alert for this happening.

Tips—Things to watch for with common ground

Some customers who know this technique get irritated with sales people who come in and want to talk about sports because they know which team their customer follows. However, during business time, that customer may not want to spend twenty minutes of their valuable time talking about their team with every sales person who comes through the door, and you might be the tenth one that day and it will one too many! If you are dealing with a new customer, it might seem like an easy option to create common ground when you feel there is none. BEWARE because this can backfire very easily on you.

Let me tell you about the account manager who was having real trouble getting a customer on side. He was a very persistent guy, showed tenacity and finally the relationship started to get a bit easier. Eventually he was able to discover his customer spent most weekends either mountain biking or white water rafting. Flushed with success at his progress, the account manager was tempted into inventing stories. He would tell tales of his own mountain biking adventures and white water rafting exploits, and for a long time it worked really well. So well in fact that eventually the customer invited him to go away for a weekend of mountain biking and white water rafting. Incredibly, the account manager was actually scared of water, and simply could not have got into that boat. This then created a hideously embarrassing situation he had to deal with. The lesson here is please don't fabricate or invent common ground if it does not exist.

It is also possible to create too much common ground with a customer and have that backfire on you too. This happened to a sales person who was selling products direct to pharmacists. With one customer, the rapport was so strong that as soon as he walked through the door the pharmacist was genuinely delighted to see him and would always sit down, have a cup of coffee and then they'd have a good conversation about the news, or sports and their rapport was excellent. However one day, after chatting for a while, the door opened and the pharmacist was called out into the store. After a few seconds he popped his head round the door and apologised but he had to go because "...there's a salesman here who wants to sell me something." The lesson here is that someone was going to make a sale, and it wasn't going to be him on that day. Excessive common ground can lead you to waste too much time with small talk instead of getting on and achieving your goals.

Matching and Pacing Top Ten Tips

In order to get really comfortable and relaxed with these techniques you need to practice regularly and these are some simple tips that will really help you to be completely natural when using them.

1. Take matching and pacing VERY slowly and focus on just one element at a time rather than trying to do everything at once. You are more likely to blow it by being unsubtle and it is also likely to confuse you if you are trying to concentrate on too many things at once.

2. Watch people from a distance in shops and restaurants and practice matching and pacing without any pressure. It will help you learn to observe the subtler signals people give out, and is a great way to practice matching and pacing body language without any comeback. You don't even have to try and communicate with them, just practice matching and pacing until you feel comfortable that you can do it subtly and naturally.

3. Then you are ready to start practising for real—just not on your customer yet! Try it with people where it doesn't matter if you get it wrong. People in bars, shop assistants,

someone at the gym, just anyone you can practice on and refine your technique until you are confident it has the desired effect.

4. Use a few seconds time lag when matching as this makes it more subtle. If you notice they've changed their posture and you think you need to change yours, don't do it immediately but count slowly to five first. Otherwise you get a 'Simon says' effect which can quickly spiral downwards.

5. In the same way, don't take mirroring to the extreme because it can get very silly as well as being obvious. Try approximating instead so if there is a large difference between your posture and theirs, by all means move closer but don't copy it exactly. If you are both leaning back and they suddenly stand up, you could try sitting up very straight rather than immediately jumping out of your chair, or if they cross their legs, cross your ankles.

6. Remember to try and pace things that are further below consciousness, as this again is more subtle. Things like breathing can be quite hard in some situations, although in a telesales context it is easier and can be extremely powerful. If you want to focus on breathing when face to face with someone, you can look for other cues such as their shoulders moving, or their chest rising and falling. Eye contact is another less conscious thing, but it must be done appropriately. Staring fixedly at your customer will probably not only make them feel uncomfortable but encourage them to doubt your sanity.

7. Make sure you calibrate properly before interpreting your customer's signals. This particularly applies to eye contact,

as it is often misquoted from popular psychology books that lack of eye contact indicates that someone is lying or avoiding. It might be either of those things, but it is more likely that it could indicate something else such as shyness or in some cultures it is a sign of respect or deference. In situations like this, where a given signal is potentially ambiguous, you need further clues in order to calibrate properly. You will find that body language tends to communicate information in clusters, so look for other signals that can validate what you are thinking.

8. Pay attention all the time. Always look at what is happening in the other person when you are using these techniques. Most of us spend a lot of our time focusing within rather than outwards and this is when we miss things. It is perfectly normal when you are learning these techniques to find them quite exhausting at first until they become more subconscious, then they will take a lot less effort. Constantly pay attention so you will avoid letting yourself slip back into Autopilot.

9. Avoid excessive rapport in a business context. Like the pharmaceutical rep who was no longer viewed as a sales person, it is not necessarily a case of 'the more rapport, the better.' Also, when you are in very deep rapport with someone, the improvement in communication doesn't only encourage transfer of ideas; it also allows values and beliefs to transfer more easily. This might sound great, but remember that it works BOTH ways so if you are in deep rapport you need to guard yourself against taking on board things that are not consistent with your goals or things that make you lose sight of them. That's why a key element to relationship building is to have well-defined goals.

10. Remember that you can break rapport as easily as you can establish it. You can break it by mismatching, whenever you need to. That doesn't mean ruining your relationship with your customer, it is sometimes essential. You may need to break whatever mood you have first established in order to be able to move on to a more useful state. For example, if you are caught up in small talk with your customer and want to move on, a small glance at your watch can break the depth of rapport and allow you to bring the conversation back round to business. Coughing, mismatching posture, altering the speed and pitch of your voice—these are all things that most of us already do subconsciously in a situation we want to change.

Finally, remember that Rapport IS NOT just about matching and pacing body language, tonality, language, beliefs and values. These are only tools to help you establish rapport with someone. Rapport IS about having—and demonstrating—a willingness to step inside someone's world and understand it from their point of view. Establishing rapport is your responsibility; it's about earning the right to lead someone else and earning it through this willingness to step inside their world. And in a sales context, the onus is firmly on the shoulders of the person who wants to do the influencing. You can't expect your customer to make this effort because the behavioural flexibility and willingness to understand must be your job, not theirs. When you can do that you have truly established rapport.

Buying signals

A quick word here about the importance of being able to know when your customer is ready to buy. They will always give off a signal that they are ready to buy, and you can close the sale. However, you need to be aware and watch for it because an inability to calibrate accurately, that is really see and notice where the customer is and in what state, is the reason so many buying signals are missed. The best example of this is when the sales person keeps on selling long after buying signals have been given off. It may not be something the customer says, it maybe an internal change in state which leads to a change in their colour, facial tension, breathing, posture, eyes moving in a different direction or breaking eye contact. It could quite literally be anything. Every thought and emotion is portrayed in some way—that's what lie detectors register as they detect the subtle changes that are continually taking place in our bodies.

A Clear Perspective

It might seem as if you have had an awful lot of information and techniques to absorb around developing rapport. Take heart, rapport is actually as natural to you as breathing and although it may seem you are juggling to keep too many balls in the air and have far too much to think about there is a great shortcut I can share with you.

As you have seen, when you want to use matching and pacing to establish rapport it involves physiology, tonality and the customer's own words, values and beliefs. These are often completely subconscious behaviours and the simplest and most effective way to activate them, and avoid feeling awkward, overwhelmed, or worried about mimicking them, is to show that you are very interested and curious about them. If you can do this then you will trigger a natural rapport building response between you and your customer. Robert

Cialdini in 'The Psychology of Influence' describes this as the Rule of Liking. It states that just sitting and finding something that you positively like about the person will generate rapport, whether that's in a business or personal context.

So, don't struggle with this, just think about how you can develop a deep state of genuine interest in them and what they want. Focus on what you like about them, and if you are doing this sincerely they will feel appreciated and rapport will follow much more naturally.

We have laid the groundwork here for great rapport building, and there are also more advanced techniques still to come around pacing and leading, and dealing with difficult or cynical customers. It's time now to look at how important it is to understand behaviour profiling. Before you read the next two chapters, remember that what you have learned so far is that if you listen carefully, your customer will always tell you what they want, and how they want you to tell them about it. If you believe in yourself, your product and what you are doing your customer will always tell you exactly how to influence them. Then all you need to do is give that back to them in your presentation. Let's find out more in the next chapter about how you can learn to recognise the signs your customer is giving you and how you can develop the sensory awareness to notice the evidence of how to influence them and to have the behavioural flexibility to respond accordingly. You are about to learn how to have an extraordinary, even unfair, advantage in selling.

Chapter Three: Behaviour Profiling

People are fascinated by people; we all wonder what makes someone else tick. In order to really understand someone in a sales context you need to know how to use behaviour profiling. Why? It's because we all have a unique perception of the world. And, in a particular context, the way in which we perceive things may be different. There is often a major difference in the way we act at home and at work, for example. Behaviour Profiling helps us understand how others see their world and predict how they may behave in a given situation. It is a skill that once learned will help you sell more effectively and avoid many of the most common problems if you can understand your customers a little better. Fortunately, you will find that your customers give away enormous clues about themselves in the way that they talk. It's not just what they say but also how they say it and a few simple questions will provide you with a wealth of information about their patterns of motivation, thinking and decision-making. Once you have that, then you can adapt your language to match them and make it much easier to persuade them.

At it's simplest, behaviour profiling involves noting the answers to a few carefully phrased questions and making some simple observations. This is guaranteed to reveal extremely valuable information about three things: what is important to them, how they get motivated and how they make decisions.

Once you understand what to look for, you can learn to tailor these questions in a way that's appropriate for both you and your customer. The most important thing you can learn about Behaviour Profiling is that it is totally dependent upon context. The pattern someone has in a particular context does NOT mean they will always behave in this way, like the example earlier about the difference between work and home behaviour. So it is important whenever you ask a question that you very clearly specify the context you are asking that question in. For example, a general question without context might be 'what do you prefer, Red or White?' but placing it in the context of what you want to know would be 'what do you prefer, Red or White wine? Context strongly influences the answer you will give to any question, and in Behaviour Profiling that applies in just the same way. The best way to explain Behaviour Profiling is to do it and to follow the process by actually asking the questions, and then to sit back and consider what the answers really mean.

What's the Benefit?

Behaviour Profiling is a skill that you need to learn and apply through regular practice and the benefits of using it are considerable. It will help you consider the effects of what you are doing and allow you to act with more precision. It will provide a framework you can follow to achieve results, or adapt to your personal style as it increases the amount of choice you have in the way you behave. It will help you achieve a gradual improvement in your performance and provide you with a radical new approach for selling successfully to more customers.

The Essential Patterns of Behaviour

There are seven key patterns of motivation or behaviour that will be of benefit to you in understanding and persuading your customers. BUT, before you start on identifying people's patterns, it's important that you understand that none of these patterns should be judged. There is no 'good' or 'bad'—in fact all behaviour does in fact have a positive intention and all patterns have different strengths and their own applications. When you start learning this it's normal to pass judgement about people's patterns, but don't worry, just be aware of it. You will often find yourself judging those you perceive to be like you more favourably, and those you perceive to be dissimilar from you more unfavourably. Finally, if you decide through this process that one of your patterns is not working for you, you will have the choice to change it if you want. And that's got to be a good position to be in.

The Motivational Direction Profile

To find out what really motivates someone there are two essential questions you want to ask. Practice this with someone and write down their answer verbatim. It is really important that you write down **exactly** what they say, so you only have their own words and not your interpretation of them.

Question: What is important to you about ....?

For example, what is important to you about a job in the context of work? or What is important to you about the computer supplier you will use for this project?

This tells you what their criteria, or values, are and can reveal what is important to them and what they perceive as important in a particular context and will stimulate a positive reaction when you use them back to your customer.

Question: And why is having that important to you?

You may get several answers when you ask the first question, and then it is useful to rank their criteria in order of importance and ask which one they would choose first.

What these questions highlight are the two ways of triggering motivation and that is either to achieve or to avoid an outcome. This is their 'direction of motivation' and what it tells you is if they are motivated towards attaining an objective, their goals, or away from a situation they want to avoid, their problems. Of course it is not that clear cut because none of us are 100% one or the other. In practice around 40% are motivated away from problems, 40% are motivated mainly towards goals and 20% are motivated by both, although one will generally be more dominant.

A towards person gets excited by having a goal; having something to get or attain. The more Towards a person naturally is, the more focused they are likely to be on their goals and be better at managing priorities. At the extreme, they may be so keen to pursue their goal that they may struggle to recognise, or just don't see, existing or potential problems that are likely to affect them and if they don't have any goals to aim for then the more de-motivated they may get. An Away From person is excited by solving problems or avoiding issues. They look for things that might go, or have gone, wrong and they get motivated by solving these problems. The more Away From they are, the more they are likely to focus on crisis management and, at the extreme, tend to focus on solving current or future problems, sometimes so much so that they can lose sight of their goals. Although they make good trouble-shooters and risk managers their attention can easily get distracted from priorities when a crisis occurs.

Motivational Direction influencing language

People may have very similar goals or ambitions at work, but it is the way they talk about them that highlights their true motivation direction. You need to be an active listener and be aware of the keywords each type will use.

Towards people use words like: gain, achieve, get, have, include and typically might say 'I want to be rewarded well and get a promotion.' To effectively influence them you need to tell them about what they will get from something, what goals they will achieve, and how it will help them achieve what they want.

Away From people tend to use words like avoid, get rid of, solve, exclude, don't get, don't want and typically might say 'I don't want to have to struggle for money and I want to avoid getting stuck at the same level.' To effectively influence them you have to focus on the situations they can avoid by doing something, and the lack of problems they will experience.

For the 20% who are equally both types they naturally will use both sets of words, and so must you. You might hear a sentence that covers both ends of the range, such as 'I want a promotion and I don't want to have to worry about money.'

Motivational Direction and persuading your customer

Now that you are aware of your customer's motivational direction you can use their orientation to influence them and make it easier to sell to them. If they are orientated **Towards** goals, positive things and pleasure then you influence them with the benefits and advantages of what you are selling. You must state it in positive terms and stress the good things that they will get when they own or have your product or service. If they are oriented **Away From** problems, pain and negative things then you influence them on the basis that what you are selling solves their problems. Emphasise how it will reduce their pain, frustrations and whatever they want to avoid.

Once you have mastered the use of the right influencing language for your customer's pattern then you have a much easier relationship with them because they don't have to get bogged down in translating what they think you mean. You will have their whole, undivided attention and your communication will make them feel like you really understand them…

WARNING. You need to be clearly aligned with your customer's orientation because if you try to persuade someone with an Away From orientation by emphasising what they can achieve or what the benefits will be, you can end up frustrating them. What they want to do is move away from problems and pain and you are talking to them about moving towards pleasure, achievement and what they will get. You are not talking their language and you are unlikely to get through to them because your words will not be reflecting their orientation, in other words you are out of alignment with them and this can easily break rapport.

Remember

Patterns are contextual and what we are looking at here is how people behave in a sales context. Just to make it crystal clear, and avoid any possible confusion around motivational orientation, be aware that Towards and Away From is **NOT** Positive and Negative and Towards and Away From is **NOT** Optimism and Pessimism. It's simply about the language that you use, normally quite unconsciously, to describe your motivation. The underlying aims may in fact be exactly the same:

- to become rich, to avoid poverty
- to get a promotion, to avoid being stuck in a rut
- to have better customer relationships, to avoid having poor customer relationships

The Frame of Reference Profile

Where does their motivation come from?

There is an essential question you must ask first, and it is essential that you note their answer **exactly** as they say it. You need to know where your client or customer's motivation to make a decision or buy from you comes from. Is it external or based on their own views and opinions?

Question: How do you know you have done a good job at work?

This question is designed to discover their Frame of Reference or the source of their motivation. What you are looking for here is whether they rely on their own judgement of their performance or decision making in the context of the sale. Do they look for feedback from others or outside sources, or is it a combination of the two? You can ask the same thing in a different way such as 'Who do you involve when you make a decision?' or 'How would you know you have made a good decision?' or 'How did you know last time you made a good decision when buying this kind of product?' and 'How would you react if someone disagreed with your decision?'

Their response will show you whether their frame of reference is internal or external and, once you are aware of which pattern both you and your customer tend to exhibit, in the context of the sales process, then you can gain the flexibility to use whichever is most appropriate for each situation. If you find yourself struggling to sell to someone, you will be able to try switching patterns and see if this has any effect. Refer back to Chapter 1, pay attention to the response you are getting and if it is not what you want then you have the behavioural flexibility to match their pattern and this relates to all patterns

Internal people are self-referencing and therefore based on their own internal opinions and view of what is right and appropriate. They are motivated to gather information and compare it against their own standards in order to make a decision. Extreme internals often cannot hear what other people are really saying or they take it as information rather than instruction. They find it difficult to be open to new ideas or to learning something new and tend to appear defensive under criticism. Internals don't do their 'shoulds'.

External people tend to base their decisions on what others think and they really need feedback or confirmation from others in order to make a decision and feel motivated. If they don't get feedback it is very de-motivating for them and if they get conflicting feedback they can be unable to make decisions. Extreme external types may take mere information as instruction and they tend do their 'shoulds'. In the context of being an external sales professional you probably get your motivation from sales reports or from your manager's feedback about your performance. External customers may get their motivation from their colleagues or manager's opinion or proof that someone else in their position made a similar decision.

Respect is also a key issue in this area. If you criticise an Internal person, they will tend to judge the other person, but if you criticise an External person, they tend to question themselves. However, this only holds true if the person who provides the criticism is someone who is respected. If you don't respect someone else, you are more likely to be internal when in context with them.

Another important element is self esteem and being External is NOT the same as having low self-esteem although the lower your self esteem the more you **may** look to others for validation. However there are plenty of Externals with high self-esteem and who have no self-esteem issues. This is simply about where you get your motivation from—is it from others smiling at you or is it from knowing inside that you've done well? This may also change as people mature within a job or role; they have a tendency to become more internal through having greater experience. This gives them more confidence to make their own decisions.

Frame of Reference influencing language

Each of the two types has their own particular requirements and you need to use the right language for each one

Influencing internals

You must provide the best information you can for them to make a decision. Inviting them to 'consider something' can be extremely powerful, they often don't want a fixed solution—they want information they can make their decision from.

Influencing externals

The focus needs to be on the positive feedback they will get from other people. They may want a one-stop solution that is guaranteed to get a good response or to achieve a certain target result. That way they will get positive feedback once they've made the decision and it will reinforce the likelihood of them coming back to you again.

Potentially externals are easier to influence, so creating a situation that encourages someone to become more external will make it easier to educate and influence them. One way to do that is by demonstrating strong credibility with your product or market knowledge. If they respect you in your field, they are more motivated to listen to your input or feedback when making a decision.

Combined patterns

Few people will be absolutely internal or absolutely external, people tend to fall somewhere on the scale and you need to decide where they are in this context. This applies to both individuals and to groups where you will have a mixture of patterns to deal with. If you are selling to a group you need to appeal to both sides and although this might sound confusing the listeners will selectively filter what they want to hear.

It is useful to bear in mind the interactions between Decision Making motivation and Direction of Motivation, as that may make certain approaches more or less successful. An example of Combined Patterns is someone who is a perfectionist and who always spots a mistake and for whom nothing is ever good enough. Even if you spend all night working on a 'perfect' sales proposal for this Internal/Away From customer, they are not going to accept it—partly because it's not been done in their way (Internal) and partly because they love to fix things (Away From).

The most irresistible thing you can offer the Internal/Away From customer is something they can fix. So you can go and see them and say 'I've produced a draft proposal on how to solve the problem we've been having but it's not perfect yet, so would you take a look at it?' Once they have had the opportunity to 'fix' any problems, and fix them to their own satisfaction, they are more likely to respond positively to it.

Frame of Reference and persuading your customer

To persuade someone who has an External Frame of Reference you need to supply as many external facts, figures, studies, opinions, references and review as possible and suggest they will get positive feedback from others once they own the product or service you are selling.

To persuade someone who has an Internal Frame of Reference you need to make it seem like it was their own idea by suggesting that they will have their own reasons for making the decision to buy your product or service. Language to convince an internally framed person will show that much of the conversation is oriented to towards **them** making the decision. You might say 'Whilst you're thinking about making your decision imagine all the best benefits of the product that you can personally see. Think about your own reasons why you really want it because it's your decision and only you can convince yourself that this is the right product for you.'

The Work Pattern Profile

How does your customer like to think or process information? Do they like lots of choices and endless options or do they like tried and tested procedures and robust processes? This question is designed to discover how someone approaches their daily work, and it will give you great insight into their preferred work pattern.

Question: Why did you choose ...your current work/your current car/your last training provider?

This question opens up a host of possibilities for you to explore because it forces people to make explicit distinctions about how they interpret the word 'choose'. Do they focus on the word 'choose', and give you a list of criteria as to why they chose their current job? Do they tell you how they got into their current job, giving you a story rather than the reasons why? Did they actively choose their job, based on the options available to them, or do they see choosing as a more passive thing, something that's part of a bigger process?

Or is it a combination of both? Are they perhaps more interested in choosing options for themselves and cutting a new path, or do they prefer to follow established procedures and see things through to conclusion?

We are again looking at two poles here; at one end are those who mainly go for options, and those who mainly go for procedures. Both extremes attract around 40% of work types each, with just 20% who are equally both.

Options typical profile

These are the original 'Why?' people and are motivated by choice. They want to be developing new options, dreaming up alternatives and exploring possibilities. Often very creative, they tend to never finish a project, but are always moving on to the next idea. They can be quite compulsive about having choice, and if you give an extreme options person a failsafe, guaranteed way to make a million pounds within one year they will change it, and try and improve on it. They just cannot leave a procedure alone, even a proven one and tend to be great at devising new procedures, just poor at following them! Having no concept of the right way to do something, they are always focused on making improvements and finding new ways to do things.

Procedures typical profile

Procedures people are motivated by finishing things, completing projects, following established processes through to conclusion. They are not really interested in 'why', but in 'how' things should be done. They like to have clearly defined beginning and end points and without that defined route, highly procedures people may get lost. At the extreme they will insist there is a 'right way' and if they lose procedure can get totally lost in a project and may have to go right back to the beginning.

If you are dealing with Equally Options and Procedures people you need to be aware that sometimes they will follow procedure and sometimes develop options so you need to know where they are in the process on the particular topic or project you are working with them on.

Work Pattern influencing language

Depending on whether your product is options or procedures based, you may have a very simple or a very hard time selling it in, unless you identify their work pattern and master the appropriate influencing language.

Options people will focus on choices in their answer, usually giving you the criteria that led them to choose their current situation. It may sound like they are giving you a list of bullet points such as 'I thought it would be stimulating and interesting, and it was well paid.' They strongly resist the concept that there could be a 'right way' to do something, so the best way to sell to them is to present them with seemingly unlimited choice and possibilities and avoid approaching them with a single solution or option as this will tend to demotivate them.

If you have to sell a procedures-based product to an options person, try focusing on the features that are customisable. Emphasise how much choice there is in the final specification and explain the different ways there are to arrive at the same result, or the shortcuts and tricks you can use to get the most out of the system. You may even focus on custom-made applications or future developments that are possible as these will appeal more strongly to them. It is most effective to talk about 'opportunities, choices, expanding, options, alternatives and possibilities' and with an Extreme type it is particularly powerful to suggest that you are 'breaking the rules just for them'.

Procedures people will focus on the events that led to their current situation, providing a story about **how** rather than why. They seem to distort the question of why and only hear 'how' and end up telling you a story. They are more likely to say something like "Well, I was completing a contract and happened to bump into someone in the same field who had an opening for someone good with figures and I was soon to be out of work, it's where I ended up." They definitely don't want to be presented with too much choice and if you do that they will get overloaded and be unable to decide. If you have to sell an options-based product to them try and elicit their criteria and then narrow down the choices to one recommendation. It's sometimes better to present a complete solution, so focus on the fact that this is the right way to do it, it is a tried and tested route that has generated good results and proved to be the best option'.

Talking to them about procedures they will get to use can be a powerful attraction for them, but even better is actually getting them started on a procedure, as they will feel compelled to finish it. Use procedural language when you speak to them, using logical time references such as 'first…then…after which.' You can try explaining that 'step one is X, step two will be Y, and step three is the final step' to complete the purchase.

Equally Options and Procedures people provide some of both and will tend to embed some criteria in a bit of a story. They might say 'I was looking for something different when I found this job on line by chance. It offered everything I wanted; variety, autonomy and good pay, so I went for it.'

Work Pattern and persuading your customer

Flexibility is the most important element when trying to persuade these customers as their thinking patterns are so different from each other you need to be able to vary your behaviour when selling to each individual.

Options orientated customer—you stress the values that will be met by them owning or having what you are selling and the opportunities and possibilities to be gained. Don't emphasise any procedures attached to buying your product or service and certainly don't make it sound like there are too many rules and regulations. These people only need the main idea and then they tend to just go for it.

Procedures orientated customer—emphasise any rules, procedures and facts because they take comfort from a structured process. They need to know that your product is tried and tested, that there is a 'right' way and that what you are offering is it.

When you are able to customise your communication to match your customer's patterns exactly it will ensure that they feel to be in deep rapport with you and very understood.

Potential problems

Due to their very different natures, it is inevitable that Procedures and Options people may find themselves clashing. Examples abound, but an obvious one is an Accountant (procedures) with her highly entrepreneurial client (options).

Or the software development team (options) and the new product launch team (procedures).

Remember, there is no 'good' and 'bad' for these two types. Options people might be great for brainstorming ideas and promoting change and creativity, but they never finish what they start. They can be a nightmare to work with on a project and nothing would ever get implemented if it weren't for the procedures people. Being flexible enough to utilise both work patterns is a distinct advantage.

The Decision Factors Profile—Sameness vs. Difference

Is your customer looking to match something they have been used to before or do they want to mismatch and have something very different? What we want to know is how much someone is motivated by change. These questions help us find out how comfortable they are with change and approximately how often they want it in order to remain motivated.

Question: What is the relationship between the kind of work you are doing today, and the kind of work you were doing last year? Or what is the relationship between the last house you bought and the one you are looking to buy now?

This will help you discover how often, and how drastic, they like changes to be. Do they like things to remain extremely stable, that is to be pretty much the same, the same but with a few small changes or is it totally different?

The majority of people fall in the middle, with some elements the same, and some elements very different. This question cleverly uses the word 'relationship' to work out how much you are motivated by change and what it does is highlight whether you perceive two situations (now and earlier) as being the same or different. If they have trouble answering, it usually comes from seeing them as totally different. After all, if they are totally different, how can there be any relationship?

Similarity versus Difference influencing language

As you might imagine, you need very different techniques to influence the different types.

Sameness people will focus on how their job is the same as the previous year. Even if they have moved jobs their answer will focus on why it's the same, for instance saying 'It's exactly the same—I'm still selling pet food to key accounts'. Influencing this group is a challenge as they are highly resistant to change. What you need to be able to do is minimise the perceived differences between your product or proposal and what they are used to. Use terms like 'same as, in common, as you always do, like before, unchanged, constant, as you know already, continue' in order to give a sense of familiarity, security and stability.

Difference people will focus on all the differences between this year and last year, even if they are apparently in the same job. They are more likely to say things like 'It's totally different. Last year I was handling basic account management but this year I'm handling much more complex promotions and customer reviews.' They are also not likely to see that there is any relationship between how things were then and how they are now. To sell effectively to them the emphasis needs to be on how the product or concept is totally different, how it will revolutionise the way they do something, or how it will make them feel completely transformed. Successful language to use includes 'brand new, totally different, completely changed, radical redevelopment, switch, shift, unique, revolutionary.'

Sameness with exception people form the vast majority of people at work and they will focus on similarities whilst acknowledging some change. You are likely to hear 'It's basically the same as last year except I have a bigger budget.' To influence them you must focus on what remains the same whilst introducing the notion of gradual improvement or incremental benefits. Avoid scaring them by talking about revolutionary 'new' products and instead encourage them with talk of gentle progression. Use language that includes comparative terms like 'more, better, less, same but, evolving, progress, improvement' are particularly effective.

Sameness with Exception and Difference people demonstrate elements of both of the above two patterns and are likely to say things like 'I've become a senior account manager through consistent sales growth and I'm now working in a radically different way with my customers.' Influencing this group means combining both the above language styles, to satisfy their desire for both evolution and revolution. If you 'mix and match' by using both the above types of vocabulary that usually produces the desired effect.

Similarity versus Difference and persuading your customers

People with Sameness pattern are looking for the same and therefore that's what you should emphasise—what is the same or similar to that which they have already had before. Simply don't point out what is wildly different, new and innovative.

People with Sameness with Exception pattern (remember this is most of us) are looking for an improved version perhaps. So emphasising what has been enhanced, or is an improvement in what they have had before will convince them.

People with a Difference pattern are looking for something completely new and even if your product or service has got many of the same features they have had before focus their attention on what is radically different, revolutionary and brand new—the more dramatically different the better.

The Convincer Pattern Profile

How does your customer get convinced and therefore come to a decision? How often do they have to experience this decision making criteria before they are convinced? This is pretty essential information if you want to learn how to convince your customers better. There are two separate questions but, depending on how someone answers, you may find you have received both pieces of information in response to the first.

Question: How do you know someone else, working in a similar role to you, is good at their job? or How will you know that the training provider you choose is the right one?

Notice how they respond. Do they talk about having to see someone in action, or do they mention hearing about them, working with them or actively participating in something with them or do they refer to needing to read something?, What you are looking for is what input do they primarily rely on when making a judgement, and next you want to know something slightly different.

Question: How many times do you have to (see, hear, read, do) something to be convinced?

They might say just once or several times and now you might want to press a bit further.

Question: How many times do you have to experience that (see/hear/do/read) to be *totally convinced?*

Often it takes some repetition before they are totally convinced and you need to know how many times it takes to totally convince them. It may take a period of time or maybe they are never totally convinced at all.

That first question establishes what kind of primary input someone needs in order to become convinced of something. It tells you which sense they primarily rely on when making a judgement and we call that the Convincer Channel. It is sensory based, through seeing, hearing, doing, or reading and in a work context more people make decisions based on what they see and hear than any other way. The second question then establishes what actually triggers someone's conviction about something. The Convincer mode is all about what it takes to get them absolutely convinced. It is loosely based on frequency which is either number, automatic response, period of time or consistency. Numbers people are only convinced after experiencing the evidence a set number of times, automatic people tend to jump to conclusions, period of time means they are only convinced once they have experienced the input for a set period of time and consistent people are never completely convinced because every day is a new day and causes re-evaluation. The majority, 52% are number people when it comes to being convinced at work. On frequency, around half of us are convinced from a certain number of repetitions, and that number tends to average out as 3 times.

Convincer Channel influencing language

Having this knowledge can make it simple to convince someone to buy from you, just follow their strategy and remember it might not be the same as your own, use your behavioural flexibility and do it any way.

If they need to **see** to be convinced think of all the things you can **show** them, certainly show them the product where possible. If they need to **hear** it may be that in addition to you telling them you get one of your already satisfied customers to **tell** them. If **doing** convinces them you might suggest a pilot project or just even giving them the product to **have and hold** and play with. Car salesmen have long known the benefits of the test drive!

If they need to **read** something, give them **written** reports or written references and endorsements from your already happy customers.

Some will make up their mind automatically but for others you will have to give them a number of examples or maybe call them a number of times before they will be convinced. Whilst yet others will need time before they are convinced yours is the right product. If you cannot be sure how they come to a decision then try one convincer pattern at a time and watch their responses.

The Activity Level Profile

This next pattern is not determined through direct questioning but instead by listening and observation. Does this person like to jump in and act, or do they prefer to first consider and wait? Do they tend to fidget and find it difficult to be still for long periods, or are they outwardly calm and content to sit back and analyse?

Activity Level observation analysis

This pattern is about the level of activity, or desire to act, in someone and has two poles; proactive and reactive. In this context they do NOT mean the same as in modern business culture. It's not just about initiating solutions before problems arise, or waiting for problems before doing anything about them. It's primarily about whether someone wants to act or to analyse. Do they want to shoot first and ask questions later—or not at all? Or do they insist on having every possible detail before they feel confident to act.

Around 15-20% of people are **Mainly Proactive** in a work context and tend to be good at going out and getting a job done. At the extreme, they may not consider anything at all and can upset people by bulldozing them. The vast majority, 60-65%, are **Equally Both** and this is a good starting assumption unless you have strong evidence to the contrary. The other 15-20% are **Mainly Reactive** and they want to understand fully before acting, but at the extreme they may operate far too cautiously, use excessive analysis and never actually 'get started'.

Activity Level influencing language

Proactive people tend to speak in crisp, clear sentences: Noun—Active Verb—Tangible Object. 'He gave me the complete report. I've read it.' They talk very directly and as if they are fully in control of their world with their words expressing actions very clearly. For example: 'I meet with my customers once a month.' Influencing mainly proactive people is easier if they think they are going to get to do something straight away, so use terms like 'do it, go for it, jump in, don't wait, get it done, now, act immediately.'

Reactive people tend to use a more rambling style of speech with longer sentences (often incomplete) that tend to be passive and cautious. 'That report was passed on to me a while back, when ...well, I've been given the chance to have a think about it...it seems to me to be fairly complete.' Their speech gives the impression the world controls them so their words indicate they are thinking and considering, cautiously, and they use lots of conditionals like 'would, could, might.' Mainly reactive people respond well to a suggestion that they are going to gain understanding from the action so use language like 'consider, analyse, think about, might, would, could, understand.'

Equally Proactive and Reactive people tend to exhibit a milder form of both behaviours, or to switch flexibly from one to the other as appropriate. Their language usually indicates both elements, for example 'I meet with my customers monthly to review their business. It's important they understand that I'm accessible.' A mix of proactive and reactive language styles works best for most people.

Activity Level and persuading your customer

Customers who are Proactive can feel like the dream clients because they can have made a decision and taken action almost before the words are out of your mouth. Reactive clients can be very frustrating, especially to the Proactive salesperson, and the key here is not to get frustrated, just understand why they are behaving in this way and stick with it

The Capacity for Detail Profile

We each hold and manage data differently and this is reflected in the way we communicate that same information to others. We each have our own personal way of chunking information to make it manageable, for instance in the way we each remember telephone numbers. This pattern is determined through listening and observation to work out what size chunks of information a person can handle well. Do they like to sit back and look at the big picture, or do they prefer to get down into the little details? Observing how someone communicates will highlight the best way to feed information back to them so it is more quickly and easily understood and assimilated. This is essential because once you know how someone takes in information you can determine the most effective style in which to present concepts, products or solutions in order to influence them.

Capacity for Detail observation analysis

Does someone give every detail or just an overview? That sums up the two opposite poles of this pattern, the specific and the general. In the work context you generally find around 15% are **Mainly Specific** and typically they handle smaller pieces of information better, treating them in sequence at a detailed level. They can find it hard to see the big picture and can lose priorities when bogged down in detail. 25% are **Equally Both specific and general** so they can naturally work comfortably in both patterns. They are capable of holding an overview and maintaining sight of priorities whilst also being able to go into an appropriate level of detail.

The vast majority, 65%, are **Mainly General** and their preference is to work at a conceptual level. They certainly can get into detail, but usually only for a short time. If it goes on too long they can get irritated and will often present ideas in random order, as they have a clear overview.

Capacity for Detail influencing language

Specific people tend to speak in sequences, moving logically from detail to detail. They communicate lots of descriptive detail and information in their speech, for example they might say 'Yesterday at 10am George and I met with Mr Vincenti, our big client from Rome, who wanted to talk about renewing our shipping contract for the third year in a row. He wants to have the price of the corrugated cardboard packaging to be included in the total price as part of the preliminary discussions for next year's contract.' Plenty of detail in there, and if you want to influence specific people it is easier if you use terms like exactly, precisely, specifically. They also like a clear, logical sequence so you must avoid jumping from one idea to another. At extremes, if you interrupt their flow to ask a question or try to move on beyond the step they are on, they will lose their place in the sequence and then have to start again from the beginning. However you can try to hurry a specific person through their detail by adding positive comments such as 'OK, and then what?' but be careful, if you push them too far, you may have to sit through the whole thing all over again.

Equally Specific and General people tend to exhibit both styles, moving flexibly from one to the other as appropriate. Their language usually indicates both elements for example they might say 'Yesterday, Mr Vincenti told George and I that he wants packaging costs included in our shipping prices for next year's contract.' A mix of specific and general language styles works best for this pattern, and although it may seem as if this pattern might be an ideal combination it can have its drawbacks. .If you think about a manager with this pattern, they will tell you not only **what** to do, but also exactly **how** to do it—in great detail!

General people form the largest group in a work context and tend to talk at overview level, summarising just the outline information required, though they may present it in a random order. Because they can see the overview at all times, they can see all the connections between the seemingly random ideas and the whole picture. Their ability to remain focused on priorities is strong, but they have little tolerance for following the detail. They use short and simple sentences, and unlike the previous examples they would probably just say 'Rome wants to renegotiate.' Mainly general people respond well to language like 'essentially, overall, in general, the important thing is the big picture, top level.'

Capacity for Detail and persuading your customer

This could not be simpler: all you have to do is simply match your customer and be like them. By being aware of the capacity for detail that your customer likes to operate with you can match them. Don't bore a big picture person with minor details and don't speak in general terms and give abstract ideas to a person that needs all the finer details to help them make a decision.

Behaviour Profiling in Practice:

This chapter has given you the information you need to acquire, or develop, new skills and tools. Everything we have learned so far is designed to be used to help you do your job more effectively. If this has all seemed like a lot to take in, here's a quick reminder of what we have covered so far.

Top tips for using behaviour profiling techniques

- Take the time to practice.
- Practise on people other than your customers to start with.
- Always pick a context first, and make sure you define it clearly.
- Start by focusing on just one pattern per week.
- Learn to adapt questions in an appropriate way for your personal style.
- Don't take too long over one question.
- When in doubt, guess and test!

Behaviour Profiling is well worth the time and effort it takes to practice.

If you get a lot of someone's patterns wrong, they will want to leave the situation as soon as possible. If you get someone's patterns mostly right, they will feel understood, connected and be more open to influence by you. You also might find it hard to get into a pattern that's totally opposite to yours. It won't feel comfortable, there will be a strong urge to get back to what you're familiar with, and you will probably at first exaggerate the traits you're not used to. This is where practice is essential in helping you get more flexible and more subtle. It can also help reduce the amount of value judgements you make about patterns other than yours.

Last word

You have learned seven persuasive patterns that will allow you to read your customer like a book. Now you understand exactly how to elicit and detect these patterns you can tailor your persuasive communication to match that of your customer. Your customer won't know why they feel so good about communicating with you and why it felt so good to make the decision to go with your product or service, but they will connect you with that feeling.

Now you are ready to learn how to identify exactly what you must offer your customer in order for them to agree to take the action you desire.

Chapter Four: Criteria Elicitation

You may be wondering why this chapter is called Criteria Elicitation and not something you may be more familiar with such as 'Questioning Techniques'.

A lot of importance is placed on questioning skills in many sales training courses and much of it is pretty irrelevant. Many people end up getting confused about what to ask and how to ask it. The most commonly used are open and closed questions where open questions usually get you lots of information whilst closed questions get very little, usually just a yes/no answer. These types of questions do have a role to play, but this distinction between open/closed ignores something more fundamental about asking successful questions.

First you need to establish whether your question is targeted. By that I mean is it designed, *really* designed, to get you exactly what you want to know? Next, are you listening effectively to the answer and paying full attention to what your customer answers and how they say it? Using TARGETED questions and EFFECTIVE LISTENING allows you to get the information from your customer that is essential to your success. What you are learning here is how to *identify* exactly what you must offer your customer in order for them to agree to take the action you desire.

Before you even start—get into the right state

If you are not in an appropriate state it is difficult to ask targeted questions.

It will also be very clear to your customer if you are asking questions because it's something you think you should do, without really being interested in the answer. To question and listen to your customer effectively, you need to be in the most resourceful state and that is one of genuine, congruent curiosity and one where you are interested and open to new ideas. You also want to ensure you trigger an appropriate state in your customer too, before beginning to question them. We have looked at this in previous chapters, but to quickly recap, you might want them to be responsive, excited, trusting, confident, open, receptive, reassured and interested.

Designing Targeted Questions

Your aim here is two-fold: to produce carefully constructed questions that give you useful information, and avoid responses that could take your call or meeting in the wrong direction. Designing targeted questions is about being absolutely clear on what you want to know about a given customer in order to sell to them effectively. So what do you really need to know about their business, their organisation, their people, in order to be able to sell effectively to them? Lots of questions will come to mind, and this can be a lot of information you might be seeking so let's simplify it. Think about not just **what** you want to know, but **when** would be the best time to find it out. Now you might assume that in your first or second sales call would seem to be sensible, but ask yourself how the

Criteria Elicitation

customer is going to feel about you if you spend the first few meetings with them focused on getting all this information. It's likely that they might be completely put off by a barrage of questions, or might not feel ready for an interrogation so soon in the relationship. So what can you do instead? What is absolutely essential to know from the first sales call?

Actually just one thing: what is it that is important to your **customer** about the product or service that you are selling? The first part of targeted questioning is all about working out exactly what it is that you want to know about their criteria for buying your product or service. There is a right question to ask to elicit this information, although you have freedom to choose the way you ask it. But the only essential thing you need is what **they** consider important because those will be their criteria for taking action, for buying your product or service.

Questions that Elicit Criteria

Now that you are crystal clear about what you want to find out, what question or questions should you ask? You know you want to identify your customer's criteria so first let me remind you of what we learned earlier—**identifying** criteria is **not** the same as **assuming** criteria. Criteria are context-dependent and a customer's criteria may well change from one context to the next—so if you sell a range of products or services, you **cannot** assume that the same criteria will apply to each one.

The design of the question you ask is absolutely critical because if you don't design and ask a question appropriately, you won't get the answer you are looking for. These are some typical examples of what happens if you ask nontargeted questions:

'Is X (e.g. colour) important to you when choosing a product?'

Typical answer is 'Yes', but what you don't know is how important it is, or whether there is anything more important, or even if this would have been in their original list. If 'No', you can cross it off your list but it doesn't really add much to what you know.

'Are Y & Z (e.g. servicing and insurance packages) of interest to you when you're buying a car?'
Typical answer is 'Yes', 'No'…or even 'Possibly' so do any of these answers tell you what will drive that customer to actually buy from you today? No, they don't.

'Are you likely to select a supplier based on their pricing?'

Typical answer is of course 'Yes', but again, what you don't know is whether pricing is their first or last consideration and what else they will base their decision on. If 'No', it tells you nothing more.

To check if you will get the kind of information you really want, put yourself in your customer's shoes. Imagine, from their perspective, what it would be like to be asked that question and how you might answer. Will your questions result in the information you really need? If not, you need to change them, and in fact there is just ONE question you can ask to find out what you want to know:

'What is important to you about xxxxx?

This question is extremely powerful because it avoids the danger of you making assumptions about your customer and provides you with clarification of what is really important to them in this context. But what if you already know your customer really, really well? What if you have been working with them for years and you already know their criteria inside out for your product?

NEVER, NEVER, ASSUME. Never miss the opportunity to ask again.

Why? Because even if you are 100% right, you will miss the opportunity to remind your customer of what's important for **them** so don't overlook the relevance of making their criteria conscious. When you bring something to the forefront of someone's mind in this way, they have to consider your question and answer consciously—rather than just giving an automatic response. What's the value of doing this? It's twofold: first it will be that much easier to show how you can meet their criteria, and second it gives THEM essential clarification of what's important to them in this context.

You cannot afford to overlook the benefit of making their criteria conscious to them because what's important here is increasing *their* conscious awareness of what is important. What works in your favour is that generally most people like to think they behave in a consistent fashion. So once their criteria are conscious, they will be less likely to contradict themselves when you remind them and can demonstrate how you can deliver against what they said was most important.

Putting it into practice

Watch what happens when you ask the **'What's important to you about xxxx?'** question. It's not uncommon for a customer to sit back in surprise and say 'Oh, well, no one's ever asked me that before…Hmmm…what **is** important to me about this…?' and you could well get a long silence as they search and search through their mind for what's important to them. PLEASE don't be tempted to prompt them because what they eventually do come up with will be a list of **their** criteria. This is what you can then use as leverage throughout your call and throughout any deal or offer you may present. Remember that human beings aren't necessarily always logical, so they may present their criteria in any order, not necessarily in order of importance. If you think you need some practice at this, then try setting yourself a target of asking 20 people for their criteria in the next week. By the time you've finished, it will be second nature!

Questions that Elicit Values

It may be a good start, but a list of criteria doesn't give you everything you need to know. Criteria are labels for underlying values, but it is often more useful in sales to understand *why,* rather than just *what* they want. Why is it important to them, why do they want it? To elicit values, you need to follow up that first question fairly smartly with this one:

'And what does having that (criteria) do for you?'

Using this question, you can keep paring down until you know you have reached 'congruent' values. You know when a customer is being congruent in their answer by noticing their

Criteria Elicitation

body language and whether it is consistent with what they are saying. The values a customer expresses in this way may give you a great insight into how else you can approach selling to them.

Everything you say and do about your product or service, once you understand your customer's values and motivation, can then be consistent with what they have told you.

Let's look at how this works in practice for a young car salesman who not only wants to sell cars, but is also targeted to sell alloy wheels to as many customers as possible.

> Two customers enter the showroom and when the salesman asks 'So, what's important to you about the car you're looking for today?' he gets this answer from Customer 1: 'It's got to be a BMW, 5 Series, in black.' And when he asks Customer 2 he gets this answer: 'It's got to be a BMW, 5 Series, in black.'
>
> Without asking any more questions, how can he successfully sell them the alloys? He can't—he has nothing more to refer to, so he needs to dig a little deeper. When he asks 'OK, and what will having a BMW, 5 series, in black, do for you?' he gets two very different responses:

Customer 1: 'Well, I'm a successful guy, I've worked hard all my life, and that success is very important to me—I think that this car will reflect it.'

Customer 2: 'I'm a family man, I've got two small children, and I know that BMWs have the highest standards of safety and road stability. My family's safety is paramount, and I know that driving them around in one of these will help them to be as safe and secure as they could ever be in any car on the road.'

Now knowing what the underlying end point values in both these cases are—Success and Safety—allows him to focus his selling in a way that he knows the customer can identify with.

For Customer 1: 'Good choice. And what you really need to finish the look is the 18-inch alloys. It is an option, but I think they set the car off well and make it stand out. It is a cut above those with standard wheels, and it really reinforces how successful you are.'

For Customer 2: 'Excellent choice. Just so you know, that car actually comes with 16-inch wheels on it. What I suggest you do is upgrade to the 18-inch alloy wheels, because they make the car stick to the road like glue. They turn this car from a great car into a track car, which is so stable at speed—which will of course provide you with that much more safety for your family.'

Here are two totally different selling approaches to customers with apparently the same three criteria, a BMW, 5 series, in black. Yet the success orientated salesman would have been much less responsive to alloys as a safety feature, whilst the family man probably wouldn't care too much just upgrading the appearance of the car.

You might not get to your customer's values straight away. This may mean you need to ask the same question more than once. Too many sales people don't bother at all: they make wild assumptions about what's important to their customer—which makes their presentations weak and therefore much less successful.

Effective Questioning Techniques

Jumping straight in, or repeating these questions too many times, to get underlying values might not encourage your customer to be forthcoming.

So how can you compel them to keep answering to the depth that you want? We have already answered this in part in previous chapters when we saw how important it is to get yourself and your customer into the right state first and in rapport with you.

If you plan questions in the right state of curiosity, ensure you are congruent when you ask them, and ensure you have established the right state in your customer, you will find you can get away with asking almost anything. Genuine curiosity is the best state for planning and asking questions and the positive customer states you want to invoke include helpful, open, trusting or confident. Even if you don't get an answer to your question, if the states are right and you have built rapport with your customer, you can avoid burning your bridges or getting kicked out of the sales call.

Use appropriate softeners

Instead, pave the way with softeners: these little phrases and stories can achieve many things, in addition to effectively getting you permission to ask your question. There are several of ways to do this and below are some examples of how scene setting, using a third party example, using humour and 'weasel' questions could all be used as softeners.

Setting the scene:

'It's really important to me to get this right, because this account is important to me as well as my company. Because

> *I'm really interested in your business and how we can serve you better, it's going to be quite important for me to ask you some questions. They'll probably be more detailed questions than you are normally asked by a salesperson. Would that be OK?"*

Faced with an introduction like this, who is going to say no?! You've made it clear you are interested in them and in helping them—it's all positive stuff. Your customer still might not answer everything in detail, but at least you can maintain rapport and won't cause offence by asking.

Using a third party example:
> *'What I tend to find is that it's really useful in some situations, and I've found it worked really well with clients similar to yourself, if I sit down with them for five or ten minutes or so and ask them a few questions. The answers give me a much better understanding of their business, and I've found it has helped me to develop their account so it becomes even more profitable for them. Do you think that would work here with you?'*

This can be equally effective, and notice that in both the first two softeners you are asking permission to ask the questions in the first place. It seems just about anything is possible when you have their permission.

Using humour:
> *'Sorry about this, I'm probably being a bit (blonde/dense/whatever works for you), but I'm finding it hard to get my head round what you need without asking a few more questions. Would you help me out here?'*

Said with a genuine laugh or a smile, this can work well when it comes to sensitive questions. It's like the Columbo

Criteria Elicitation

effect—act stupid in order to get permission to keep asking questions until you get what you want.

Weasel questions:

'I'm curious, I wonder, how would you feel if I were to ask you some questions about your turnover? I wonder, what would you say if I did that?'

These questions are approached as if the person is not actually asking the question at all—just finding out how you might feel if they were to ask them. They haven't asked, and perhaps they're not going to, but how would you feel if they did?

Softeners allow you to build and maintain rapport whilst interspersing them with targeted, business-related questions. These techniques can also raise your credibility by demonstrating that you are genuinely interested and care about your customer and how they feel.

Use gentler question words

Another way to soften the impact of the question you are asking is to think carefully about the language you are using. It is a fact that some people find the question WHY? very intrusive, overbearing or confrontational, particularly early in a relationship or if they have just revealed something they feel is sensitive. It might get a defensive reaction rather than eliciting the deeper information you want. Try phrasing your open questions so that they start with WHAT or HOW instead. So that instead of saying 'Why is that important to you?' try changing it to 'What does that do for you?' instead. If you are selling custom kitchens don't ask the customer 'Why do you want a granite-topped kitchen' turn it into 'What is it that makes you want a granite-topped kitchen in particular?' or 'How does having a granite-topped kitchen work for you?

This is not changing it to the wrong question—they are still effectively targeted but are less challenging for many people to answer.

Why bother to elicit criteria?

You may be wondering if it's worth the trouble of clarifying what is important to someone and why. Well, ultimately, if your product delivers in all areas then it might just be a simple case of job done—you just have to explain how your product meets their criteria and then close the deal. It's often not that easy, but it just might be. However when it isn't that simple then all these questions we have looked at are designed to identify key information that you can use throughout the sales call as well as throughout your presentation. So, if you can give your customer their criteria, do it and you can use that as leverage throughout your sales presentation.

Working out a hierarchy of criteria

Just knowing their criteria isn't always enough, you also want to be able to identify which criteria are essential and which are nice-to-haves. You also need to have a plan for what to do if you can only meet some of their criteria. Well, you can certainly still leverage those by referring back to them at every opportunity during the call and also when you are presenting your product or service. You might be fortunate and be able to meet the most important ones. This is quite key—if you can meet the top three, you could still have a good chance of a sale. It depends on knowing the ranking.

How do you work out what's most important?

There are two techniques for this, and you already have some experience of this because in the chapter on Behaviour Profiling we looked briefly at how to rank criteria in order of importance. That way involved pairing each of the criteria with each of the others, and asking the question:

'If I could offer you a product with X and a product with Y, which would you choose?', so that by pairing each one you get the customer to choose their preference and you can work out the overall ranking. The drawback to this is that it can take quite some time and unless done very smoothly, might make it rather apparent to an astute customer that you can't meet all their criteria. So what can you do instead?

Listening is the key, and you have to listen very carefully to *exactly* what they tell you. What to look for is when they use phrases like 'I need', 'I absolutely must have', 'It's got to be', 'I'd like', 'I prefer', 'It's essential' because the language that someone uses when listing their criteria will usually indicate their importance to them. These 'qualifiers' may reveal whether something is a necessity or a possibility. You are only ranking these based on the language and relative emphasis that your customer places on each criterion, not based on how you would define each qualifier. Unlike pairing which is slow and clumsy, listening is both subtle and instant.

How it works in practice

Let's say you are buying a house and the estate agent's first question is 'What's important to you in the house you want to buy?' What they will be listening for is replies like 'Well, it **absolutely has to be** in the right area...

…and we **need** a 4th bedroom……..and **ideally we want** a large garden…

…I'd **like it to be** Victorian because I love those large rooms…And of course, it's **got to be** within our budget.'

You can see from this example that the customer is using language that qualifies how important each criterion is—it's not just about word order. It's also about the emphasis that they place on each qualifier. When ranking these, it is highly likely that the order would be as follows:

Absolutely has to be would come first

Got to be is second

Need is third

Ideally we want is fourth, and

Like it to be comes last

Given the odds, it's unlikely that the estate agent will have exactly what you are looking for. But, understanding the priorities in a little more detail may help him to still make a match. So far, he probably has a fairly good idea of which criteria are absolute necessities and which are possibilities. That tells him where there may be room for negotiation. Asking what each criteria does for you will enlighten him as to your values, whilst reinforcing his judgement about the hierarchy of criteria. Again this is what he is listening for:

'The whole point of moving is so the children can attend the right school, so it has definitely got to be in the catchment area. We need the 4th bedroom because we're about to have another child, and we'd ideally like a larger garden so all the kids can play at home rather than going to the play ground. I like the feeling of space that Victorian houses give, and it's got to be within budget or we can't afford to move.'

Criteria Elicitation

By picking up on all the clues he has just been given, the agent now has all the information he needs to pitch a fairly suitable house. Given what he now knows, he might say 'Well, it's definitely in the location you want for the school—it's in the same road. There are four bedrooms, which caters for your growing family. The garden is probably not as large as you'd ideally like, but it does provide somewhere safe for the kids to play. It's not Victorian but it is 1940's so it has the large rooms that you like, and the great news is, you can get all that within your budget. Are you interested?'

Clear Criteria and PARROT Phrasing

It would be a very unusual customer who wouldn't be interested after the agent had so clearly demonstrated that he had heard what they wanted and got their criteria so accurately. How did he do it?—By listening with real attention and by using PARROT phrasing. We talked about this in chapter 3, and you will remember that it is essential when repeating someone's criteria back to them that you use exactly the same language. Make sure you are extremely precise and ensure you use exactly the same qualifiers as your customer when talking about their criteria. The same applies to repeating back their qualifier for a criterion. PARROT phrasing is the key because when they say '…and it's **got to be** within my budget' and if you are not listening properly and respond with 'OK, so you'd **like** it to be within your budget, then you are likely to get the sharp response…' 'No, you're just not listening to me—it's **GOT to be** within budget!' PARROT phrasing avoids misunderstanding and makes your customer feel listened to and valued.

Remember that Qualifiers mean different things to different people

When developing the hierarchy of someone else's criteria, make sure you look at the criteria relative to each other. Simply listening to someone's language in isolation and using that to define what is important, means making dangerous assumptions. Each qualifier can mean something very different to each of us. When someone qualifies what they are saying they are also indicating whether or not they are prepared to negotiate. This is the difference between necessity and possibility—what is untouchable, what is persuadable. It doesn't matter what word they use for necessity, but it means it is *essential*. Possibility is more about 'I'd love to'. But that could be 'in an ideal world', or 'with a fair wind blowing', or 'if I already had everything else that I need.'

So you must make sure you calibrate this based on someone's tonality, body language, etc. Look at how they talk about their criteria. What gestures and facial expressions do they use for further emphasis? This is as important as what they say for you to get the whole picture.

7 Common Obstacles to Effective Questioning: *and how to overcome them*

When you start using Effective Questioning techniques you may not find it all going smoothly. Usually this is due to running into one of the most common obstacles that you might encounter. These could be: being in an unresourceful state, lack of planning, having limiting beliefs, inappropriate questions, excessive rapport, ineffective listening and of course lack of rapport; so let's look at them in more detail and see how you can overcome them.

1. Being in an un-resourceful state:

The importance of state starts right at the beginning of the process. Remember—you cannot NOT communicate and so if you are in a state that is not resourceful when planning, your questions may not be effective. If you are not genuinely interested in your customer's answers, it will show. If you feel nervous about your right to be asking the question, it will be obvious. If you jump right in without establishing the right state in your customer, you may get such a negative response that you can't even revisit it again later.

Remember—by ensuring both you and your customer are in the right state, and by building rapport before you start, it seems you can get away with asking just about anything. Remind yourself that a quick way of getting rapport is to develop a state of intense interest in the person you are trying to build rapport with and do all you can to achieve that.

2. Lack of planning:

If you are not absolutely clear on what you want to know before you start, you won't be able to stay focused in your questioning. Without planning, a sales call could head in the wrong direction. Worse, your customer may even take the lead and you'll leave without having achieved anything.

Planning questions follows the same kind of principles as goal planning, which we have already covered in Personal Success Strategies in Chapter 1 but let's recap:

1. Before planning the targeted questions you need to ask, get yourself into the right state.

2. Once you are feeling truly curious, you can think about the information you really want to know.

3. Then work out how you are going to get it. What questions will elicit the information you are after?

4. In order to validate the questions you devise, switch to the state you are going to elicit in your customer and put yourself in their shoes. How will they perceive your questions—and what are they likely to answer? Is it the information you want?

5. Based on what you have found out, make any alterations necessary to your questions.

3 Limiting Beliefs:

Closely related to your state are the limiting beliefs you may hold. Limiting beliefs can have a powerful negative effect on your ability to sell successfully. If you don't think you can, chances are you will prove yourself right! The first stage is recognising the beliefs for what they are because until you do you can't change them or successfully counter them. Once you remove those limiting beliefs, you can plan questions more effectively. Limiting beliefs can take many forms, so do you ever find yourself thinking any of the following?

'I've no right to be asking that'

'They'll never answer that question'

Criteria Elicitation

'They're bound to say that price is important and my product is too expensive'

'I can understand why they're not going to want this product'

'If I ask that, they'll take it the wrong way.'

It helps to think about ways in which you could prepare your customer for the questions you want to ask. For instance, **what kind of softeners** might be appropriate in their case? More importantly, think about a set of **circumstances under which your customer would be interested in buying** your product and then **be creative** in thinking of a reason for them to buy.

Then, by planning effectively, target your questions to create a context in which your customer can then acknowledge there is a niche for your product.

Let's look at how this might work in practice with an example:

A team of salesmen are selling products into chemists and their usual products are items they call 'pound lines' i.e. items that cost less than a pound, baby care, health and beauty. A new product, a mousse for treating nappy rash is causing them a problem and when asked what the problem was, they answered that it was a pharmacy product not an OTC (over the counter) product and it's much more expensive than the rest of their range and competitor nappy rash products. There are several limiting beliefs operating there and this meant they were having trouble asking the kind of questions that would get them a sale. What specific questions could they ask to improve their chances? Let's break down those limiting beliefs one by one.

123

Limiting Belief 1:

Normal Nappy Cream is £1.50 a pot—what young mum is going to want to spend £.7.00 on a mousse instead?

Ever been around a screaming baby? Well, try thinking about what happens when Nappy Cream doesn't work and the mother is at her wit's end. Are you still sure she wouldn't pay £7.00 for something that works?

Limiting Belief 2:

The pharmacist won't want to stock a £7.00 product when the competition costs less than £2.00

OK. So what does the pharmacist do, when Nappy Rash Cream doesn't work? He probably sends the young mum to the doctor, because he doesn't know what else to suggest. But this product actually gives him another opportunity to make a sale, and this time a sale with a healthy profit. It also means he is seen to provide a better service than simply sending young mums off to the doctor.

Having addressed what the limiting beliefs actually are; now you can start to formulate much better questions to be asking the pharmacist. This would be a much more effective sequence of questions to use:

'When Nappy Cream doesn't work for children with nappy rash, what's your next step?'
'I send the mother off to the doctor.'
'Why do you send them there?'
'Well, because I haven't got anything else any more effective than Nappy Cream, so I think if the product is causing them a problem that's what I suggest.

'Well, here's a product that you can sell when Nappy Cream doesn't work—before you send them to the doctor. The great thing is, it gives you another opportunity to help your customers, another opportunity to make a sale and another opportunity to make more profit.'

What pharmacist wouldn't want that? That's the power of removing limiting beliefs. But remember that your limiting beliefs tend to predetermine the questions you ask, so if you went into this situation and said 'So, is price important to you in a nappy rash product?' Who is going to say no?! If you don't address a limiting belief, it will turn into a self-fulfilling prophecy because those beliefs will definitely reduce the effectiveness of your questions.

4   Inappropriate Questions:

Inappropriate does not mean that you were asking the wrong **type** of question, but simply that it was not designed to elicit the actual information you want to know. Inappropriate questions either don't get you the information you want, or in some cases can even reduce your chances of making a sale.

The best example is raising the issue of price in a closed question. If you ask 'is price important to you?' they are naturally going to say yes it is, because what customer is ever going to say it isn't? You have asked a question designed purely to confirm or deny information you have assumed about your customer. This question is inappropriate because it tells you nothing useful. An appropriately targeted question to ask is:

Q: 'What's important to you about this type of product?'
A: 'Well, it's got to be a sure fire fast seller, it's best if it's avail-

able in small pack sizes to start with and of course I'd like guaranteed availability when I order it.'

You now have a useful response that gives you plenty to work with. Remember—*you* get to choose your questions so choose wisely!

Assuming price as a criterion:

Sometimes we make assumptions based on what we believe to be true, and many salespeople believe that price is (or will be) the major obstacle to selling their product or service. This belief often comes from asking inappropriate questions, so to test this belief, Professional Excellence (the author's training company) did some research with a team of key account managers and their customers. They asked them 'What is important to you in a pharmacy wholesaler?' Now what most customers provided was between one and three criteria and 18 different criteria were given in total, including Service, Availability, Ease of Ordering, Local Representatives and Price. The results surprised them because Price was NOT at the top of most customers' lists. Only 36% mentioned it as a first priority and in fact almost half of their customers, 42%, didn't mention it at all! So if your customer doesn't feel price is the most important factor, then why should you?

5 Excessive Rapport:

Excessive rapport can, as covered in Chapter 2 on Relationship Building, lead at best to wasted time and at worst to you identifying too strongly with your customer to sell effectively to them. Of course there is nothing wrong with planning questions that are purely designed to build rapport. In

Criteria Elicitation

fact there are some customers that may require real focus in this area. But you need to do a sense check and ensure that rapport-oriented questions are interspersed with questions targeted to drive forward your business as well as your relationship. Used successfully, questions designed to build the customer relationship can also lead you more easily into the business related questions you need to ask—they can act as Softeners.

So you must ask yourself whether your questioning is achieving the results that you wanted. Targeted questions can of course achieve two types of result: building relationships and being productive in a business sense. It is easy to concentrate so hard on building rapport—or perhaps get in such deep rapport—that you neglect to ask the questions that will develop your business.

Remember: rapport building is a means to an end, and that end needs to remain clearly in your mind for you to avoid losing direction. Provided you are clear on your business and relationship aims with a customer, you can balance your questions to achieve your goals and avoid wasting yours, or your customers, time.

The aim is always for you to stay in control, so be careful because when rapport is too deep you may lose that control. If you hand control over to your customer voluntarily, the effect is exactly the same as if you lost control through inappropriate questioning. It will be that much harder to ask your carefully planned targeted questions and you've missed an opportunity.

So now you and your customer are in the right state and you've asked your targeted, appropriate and balanced questions. Is that all there is to it?

6 Ineffective listening

No, there is still more to do, because there is no point in going to all this effort if you don't also choose to listen effectively to the answers you get. Naturally we all think we listen effectively, but one of the biggest mistakes a salesperson can make is to listen and be thinking about how they are going to respond. Listening with intent to the answer in this way has several effects, none of them what you want.

First, you will be focusing on your beliefs and not theirs. You are already making some assumptions about what someone is going to say and how you should be responding to it. And that takes you back onto dangerous ground.

Second you will find it hard to PARROT phrase. You are already formulating the language that you are going to use, instead of picking up exactly the phrases and expressions that have obvious meaning for your customer.

Third it is easy to miss their non-verbal signals. You are occupying your conscious mind with how you will deliver your own response rather than watching your customer's body language for clues about their state and the congruency with what they are saying.

Finally it may change your state. Listening with intent to answer is also often quite obvious. You will not be giving out signals of congruent curiosity to your customer because it isn't your real state. They might feel, before you even open your mouth, that what they are saying isn't important to you and that you won't understand them.

You **must** pay close attention to **what** your customer is saying, and also **how** they are saying it. So what could you do to help you listen, or demonstrate you are truly listening, whilst your customer is speaking? We'll you can actively demonstrate that you are giving them your full attention, by reflecting their language back to them through PARROT phrasing or being willing to take notes—it shows you care and are taking them seriously.

7 Lack of Rapport

We have covered how important rapport is in effective communication. When rapport builds up barriers come down. If you want congruent well thought out answers to your questions, then rapport is essential.

The Rule of Three

Everything to do with Criteria Elicitation comes back to this foundation:

- Know what response or information you want to get and apply the question appropriately

- Check whether the answer is congruent by paying attention to what is said and also how it's said

- If you didn't get what you wanted, have the flexibility to ask a different or clarifying question to get it

So, let's recap on how you can really ensure that you do this effectively. First, get into the right state of genuine curiosity about your customer, really take time to listen, don't rush them and never speak before they have finished—they want to be understood, not advised. Do give subtle positive responses to their words, like a small smile or nod and listen carefully for their message, their exact words, and their non-verbal cues. It can be hard to concentrate so if your mind starts to wander, actively refocus on your customer and please don't pass judgement at this stage—it could show in your state. Do make a quick note to remember a point you want to make, but don't write so much you get distracted from listening.

In the next chapter we are going to focus on presenting your product or service to your customer. The best of the best will always ensure that the presentation is tailored to the individual and not a stock presentation that is given to everyone. To do this you need to elicit their specific criteria and use them to focus your presentation on them.

Chapter Five: Presenting

Now it is time to pull together everything you have taken the trouble to find out about your customer and use it in a powerful way. This is your opportunity to discover how to make your sales presentations more irresistible and compelling than ever before, in order to get the kind of reaction you want from your customer. When talking about Presenting in this context, it's not the big formal pitch, when you stand up in front of a large group of people and use a projector or other visual aids. This is the kind of presenting that you do every day whenever you introduce yourself, your company, a new idea, a product, a piece of work, or a deal. Not quite as big and glamorous as the big pitch but it's just as vital to get it right.

So what can we do to significantly improve your sales presentations? What, exactly, can I teach you that will make such a difference? Well, there is one technique that it seems is guaranteed to give you complete control over your sales call, every time. And it's so powerful that you'll start to see the difference the very first time you use it. If you are a seasoned sales professional, you may be thinking…'but I've been doing this for years! I'm pretty good at it, so how can you teach me anything I don't already know?' Well, some of what I'm about to share with you isn't new and you probably do these things already. What I am pretty sure you won't be doing, is putting them together in the right way.

What do I get?

What I can promise you is that although you probably have many of the ingredients I am about to share with you, you will benefit from having a recipe that's guaranteed to work. And I'll even throw in a number of extra spices you can use to begin making your presentations have even more impact. Is it really that easy? Yes it is, but in order to use these techniques successfully you will need to plan in advance and of course to practice what you learn. When you do that, it will start to become second nature and although you will still need to plan, the technique will kick in automatically so that, when you need it, you'll find your language starts to flow effortlessly. These techniques apply to every aspect of presenting to your customer and this is what we are going to look at:

Getting in control of your sales calls and keeping it. The importance of adapting to your customer's communication style. How to powerfully structure your sales presentations and how to use influencing language to mesmerise your customers, using their criteria and values to make everything you say far more compelling.

Set-Ups: Verbal Pacing and Leading

The first and most powerful techniques I want to share with you is sometimes ominously referred to as a set-up. It is more accurately called verbal pacing and leading and is similar to the non-verbal pacing and leading that you use to build rapport. A Set-up uses language to pace and lead and prepares your customer to be persuaded easily. Set-ups are a fantastic way to introduce a sales call and can form a verbal agenda. They can be used to 'chunk' parts of a negotiation and set-up any and every piece of influence or persuasion

Set-ups follow a simple 3-step structure, and it is one that seems to work perfectly if you work within the structure. This pattern fuses the most powerful language in persuasion and it is so fundamental to being a successful sales professional, that you will find mastering it more than pays for the time it takes to learn.

Never go into a sales presentation without a Set-up

This not only applies to every sales call but any presentation within a call and even if you have already done a set-up for your introduction, you can still use the same pattern again to set-up your actual presentation or chunk phases of a negotiation. Every successful Set-up involves 3 elements:

Verbal Pacing—using Truisms
Verbal Leading—using Presuppositions
And Inoculating—which is handling objections ahead of time

A Set-up can and does form the basis of a verbal agenda so make sure you never go into your sales call without a set-up prepared.

Step 1: Verbal Pacing

As usual you need to be in the right state before you start in order to build rapport. Verbal pacing is all about language and it involves using TRUISMS with your customer. A truism is any statement that is *irrefutably* true and known to be true to both parties. What you are actually doing here is pacing your customer's reality. If you say things that you both know are true, your customer has to agree with your comments because you both know it will be true.

Please note that: Using truisms properly requires planning and practice. If you don't plan carefully, you might say something that can be refuted by the customer, which breaks the pattern. You need to choose statements of truth that will create the right state in your customer. They also need phrasing in the right language because if you say something in the wrong language for your customer, it might appear untrue to them. In short, go back to parrot phrasing and use your customer's own words and phrases, the ones they habitually use.

Truisms do four useful things: They elicit a positive state in your customer; they direct the conversation towards your desired outcome, build and help maintain rapport and finally they build Response Potential which increases the likelihood of your customer agreeing with your proposal.

What kind of truisms can you use?

Truisms can relate to just about anything, although should naturally be pitched positively. Make them as specific as you can, focused on the context of your sales conversation. Specific truisms could be about your last sales call, another previous sales call, an earlier deal, a previous agreement or events in common. If you are meeting the customer for the first time, or your history is not positive, you can use more general truisms—that is things that would be true for anyone

Presenting

in that situation, not just this particular customer.

General truisms could be well publicised facts about market trends, recent events in their company, well known industry news, relevant legislation, or anything that seems appropriate in the situation.

Finally, if using general truisms doesn't look possible, you can also go one step further and use global truisms. These are universal truths that anyone would agree with such as 'world peace would be great thing'.

The more times your customer agrees with your truisms, the more likely they are to say 'Yes' when it comes to the sale. You can further increase your Response Potential by having a slight, almost imperceptible, nod of your head when you state your truisms, and just watch them nod back. Their response can be quite subtle—you don't have to get them to repeatedly say 'Yes' out loud just observe whether they are nodding or using other congruent body language as this can indicate agreement and shows their response potential is building.

Step 2. Verbal Leading

The next step is to move from pacing to leading, and this is a bit like moving from the past or present into the future. Instead of only truisms, you now start to introduce PRESUPPOSITIONS—statements of what you believe *will* be true. In this case, it is a statement of what you believe your customer *will* get as a result of your sales call, literally—you are telling them 'What's In It For Them' (WIIFM). Having reminded them of what **is** true, you now need to link those truths with what you want them to **believe to be** true. Let's see how your conversation with your customer would go to smoothly link truisms into presuppositions, from agreement in specifics to reminders of current truth to a statement about what you believe to be true:

'You'll remember it's exactly a month to the day since I was here last time. We had a talk about a few products and, I think it's fair to say, you had a few concerns about whether it would be the right thing for you to do? But we had a discussion around it and as I remember, after our discussion you took the products. And as I can see from your stock, they've already all gone.

Which I think you'll agree means that it was a great deal and it worked out exactly as we said. Now today, I've got another great deal for you, with two products that are very similar, but which will actually deliver you more profit on return than last time.'

Layering presuppositions:

To be successful, it's important to make sure you layer your truisms and presuppositions in the right way. Start off with just truisms, and then gradually build in more presuppositions, and reduce the number of truisms: You might find this table useful to remind you of how the sequence needs to go.

1   Truism Truism Truism Truism Truism Truism (6) Presupposition (1)

2   Truism Truism Truism Truism Truism (5) Presupposition Presupposition (2)

3   Truism Truism Truism (3) Presupposition Presupposition Presupposition Presupposition (4)

4   Presupposition Presupposition Presupposition Presupposition Presupposition

This pattern is effective because it's seems that our conscious mind can only handle a limited number of pieces of information at one time. Research has suggested that this may be between 5 and 9 pieces if information. Therefore consciously it becomes difficult to differentiate between what is irrefutably true and what may well be true in the future. Using this language pattern is hypnotic because you are literally communicating with both their subconscious and their conscious at the same time and it becomes harder for someone to distinguish what's true from what you want them to believe to be true.

Step 3. Inoculating

If you understand your customer, their business or the marketplace well, you may be aware of specific objections or issues that are likely to be raised in this context. If you know they will be raised at some point, why wait? If you don't handle them now, an objection could lurk in the back of your customer's mind throughout the rest of the sales call like white noise, reducing their ability to pay attention to what you are saying. So, handle the objection yourself and do it in a way that allows you to immediately counter it. Raising and handling likely objections in advance is called inoculation. It allows you to subtly clear the obvious negatives, *before* you get into the bones of your presentation. **However,** make sure any objections you plan to inoculate against are genuine objections, that is that they are very likely to be raised, and not some obscure objections that the customer may never have thought of.

With this third element in place, the language pattern then could start to look like this: Although it is important to know that you can place an inoculation just about anywhere in a set-up.

Pace, pace, pace, pace, pace—lead, lead

Pace, pace, pace—lead, lead, lead,—inoculate

Pace, pace—lead, lead, lead—inoculate

This is just a guide to use until it feels natural, why not have a go and write a set-up for yourself?

Inoculations can have other benefits. They can help build rapport by pacing the customer's concern, build credibility by showing them that you appreciate the wider context of your product and any potential issues and finally it develops trust as you are honest enough to acknowledge issues, but equally able to set their mind at rest.

Different types of Inoculation

There is some flexibility in how you can go about inoculating against something and you can employ either direct or third party inoculation.

Direct is where you meet the objection head-on and bring it out into the open so you can allay it. You might say to your customer

"I don't know, but you might be thinking at this point that it's going to be expensive, let me reassure you that it will not prove to be too expensive."

"You might be thinking that you don't have time for doing

this, can I reassure you that this will actually save time in the long run."

Third Party, as you might imagine, is a bit more indirect and this is one of the few times you can use humour, depending on the context. It might sound a bit like this:

'You won't believe this, but there some of my customers thought that they were going to have to buy a warehouse full of this! They were about to turn down this great level of profit on these products, just for the sake of taking a little bit of extra stock. Can you believe some people would think like that?'

If humour isn't your thing, then you might try this more straightforward approach.

'Some of my customers have been quite clever with this deal. They were initially concerned about taking extra stock, however soon realised that it might take up a bit more space in the short term but because it's such fast turnover the profit is more than worth it.'

Exercise: Start thinking of examples of Inoculations that would be most appropriate for use with your existing customers or for clients in the context of a sales call.

Tips on Set-ups

This 3-step pattern of Verbal Pacing, Verbal Leading and Inoculating will consistently enable you to set-up your call or presentation in a way that will make it as irresistible as possible. Your customers will respond to you in a much more positive way and you will also notice your confidence increasing with every successful call you make in this way.

Although Set-ups are incredibly simple to use, they do require **planning** to be effective. This isn't something to rush or skimp on so set aside enough time, get in the right state, and plan a detailed set-up that's specific to each customer.

Make it easy on yourself

One way to make your set-up as smooth as possible is to base it on a typical opening conversation you would have with that specific customer. That way, you can lead the call as naturally as possible. Another helpful aid is to have an agenda so that if you feel the call slipping away from you, you can bring it back on track with the agenda. Do this consistently and your customers will come to expect an agenda and it will be easier for you to stay focused.

WARNING: I do want you to be aware that:—

As with any of the techniques in this book, you need to use your integrity when applying this to a customer. What you are using here is—very powerful hypnotic language and if your product or service is of no discernible benefit to them, then using this technique to get the sale might simply make your customer develop 'buyer's remorse'. This is counterproductive for long-term relationships and so Set-ups and other hypnotic language patterns should only ever be applied when there is a clear win for your customer too.

The 4Mat System

The next tool I want to share with you is the 4Mat system. This gives structure to your presentation so that it can be understood by the greatest number of people as possible. It originated from a study of learning styles in children by Bernice McCarthy, who noticed that when she was teaching in schools children learned in different ways. As adults we all learn in many different ways, but maintain a preferred style of learning, which is the one that we find the most comfortable for our way of working.

What we have here are the four preferred learning styles that the majority of the population fall into.

4Mat	Learning Style	Percentage
Why?	Discussion	35%
What?	Teaching	22%
How?	Coaching	18%
What If?	Self—discovery	25%

"Why?" People

This group learns best by discussing the reason why and they need to know why something is worth doing or learning. They also have a need for exploring the reasons why before they will take action. "Why do we need to know this information about presenting?" or "why should I bother using this system in my presentations?"

"What?" People

This group learn best when you give them information and data, either orally or in writing. They need masses of facts, figures and statistics to be convinced so using graphs and analysis in your presentations would work for these people.

"How?" People

This group learn best by doing, and have a very hands-on approach. They need to know how you are going to go about doing whatever it is that you are talking to them about. They are not as worried about the theory or the reasons why; they just want to know how it will be done or how they will do it.

"What if?" People

This group want to know the benefits and payoffs of taking action and are also motivated by knowing the consequences of not taking action. They might be asking "what are the opportunities for me with this product?"

Addressing all four categories

In any presentation you will undoubtedly have people from all four categories so it is best to structure your presentation to meet all four styles. The question is though, what order should you structure it in? Here's the order that works best:

- Why?
- What?
- How?
- What if?

It seems this order works best because unless you give the "why" people a reason for them to be interested in your offering then they will not engage in your presentation. So it's best not to start with loads of "What" detail, because it will be wasted on the "why" people who haven't yet become interested. Give them a reason and start with why to get them motivated. Then give some of the "what?" information.

Presenting

Obviously people need details about your offering, products or service before they will take any action. Next give them the "how". Explain how they will be able to use or implement what it is you are offering them, in their context. Lastly give them the benefits and or consequences. What would happen if you did this—what would happen if you did not?

Your sales presentation

So that's the theoretical order, how would you do it in practice? Well firstly let me slightly contradict myself. Your presentation needs to start with what we might call *"little what"*. I might say to a client. "Today I want to talk to you about Advanced Sales Development System" *(Little what)*

Now you are ready to tell them why you want to tell them about Advanced Sales Development System.

"This is why you would want to know about this" or "This is why we have developed this product/service" or "This is why we have targeted your business". Now comes the main 'what' or the detail.

"This is what it is and here are the details" or "This is what we can actually do for you and here is our evidence". Moving on to 'how' with "This is how it will work for you" or "This is how you can use this in your business and this is how it will deliver the results". Finally, go for the 'what if' with "And these are the benefits you will see" or "The consequences of not doing this are…"

Of course to make this work you have to do some preparation and actually design your presentation to fit this 4Mat. You might also want to consider shifting perceptual positions when you are preparing your presentation and put your self in the customer's shoes so you **can** prepare your presentation with some insight into your audience's perspective.

Influencing Language for Presenting

So far we have looked at two ways to structure your sales presentation. What I would like to focus on now is actual language you use. The first thing to remind you of here is do not forget the power of parrot phrasing. You will find it is particularly useful when you are stating truisms. The more you reflect your customer's own choice of language, the more easily your truisms will be accepted and it will increase the depth of rapport. You are not working in the dark here. You have already done much of the hard work and have the information you need from your customer's behaviour profile. If you are not sure then take a moment now to refer back to Chapter 3. You can tailor the language you use in you're sales presentations, to their particular Behaviour Profile and use your behavioural flexibility and adopt their communication style. Here is a brief reminder of the kind of language that works well for each profile:

Motivational Direction (Towards / Away From)

Towards: (Motivated to achieve things and to attain goals) Attain, obtain, have, get, include, achieve, win, reach, gain, add, etc.

Away from: (Motivated to avoid undesirable situations and solve problems) Avoid, steer clear of, not have, solve, get rid of, exclude, away from, prevent, lose, discard, be free of, etc.

Frame of Reference (Internal / External)

Internal: (Make decisions based on their own internal standards) You might want to consider, only you can decide, it's up to you, what do you think, a suggestion for you to think about, ultimately you'll know what will work best for you, etc.

External: (Needs outside feedback or standards to make decisions)

The feedback you'll get, the quarterly sales results you'll see, so-and-so thinks, the approval you'll get, others will notice, this reference/testimonial/study shows, etc.

Work Pattern(Options / Procedures)

Options: (Like to develop their own choices)

Develop in a new direction, I'll break the rules just for you, you can choose how to adopt this, there are lots of options, you can customise it, it provides several alternatives, many possibilities, plenty of opportunities, etc.

Procedures: (Like to follow and complete a set procedure)

This is tried and tested, we have found that the best way to do this is, firstly…then…after which, it's a well-established system, simply follow the step-by-step instructions, go logically from stage to stage, ensure the project is completed on time, etc.

Decision Factors (Sameness / Difference)

Sameness: (Like the world to stay the same)

It's the same as, they have this in common, you can still do it the way you've always done, just like before, unchanged, as you already know, totally familiar, stable, etc.

Sameness with exception: (Like gradual evolution)

It's the same except, the product has evolved, developing, more, better, improved, gradually progressing, less, increasing, decreasing, same but with a few additional features, essentially similar, etc.

Difference: (Like constant and drastic change.)
Brand new, totally different, revolutionary, unique, changed, completely redesigned, started from scratch to develop this, switched, shifted, unrecognisable, a million miles away from, like chalk and cheese, etc.

Sameness with exception and difference: (Mix of the above two)

You can choose elements from either of the above; the language from both will work successfully.

How are they convinced?

Remember also how your customer becomes convinced—you can remind them of what they have heard, seen, or done as part of your Set-up truisms.

You can also build in what they *will* hear, see or do in your presuppositions. And inoculate against anything negative that they might expect to hear, see or do as a result of your sale. Your style of presentation should continue in the same vein.

When are they convinced?

Your presentation should also include how much/how often they need to see, hear or do something to become convinced. In your truisms, you can refer to the length of a trial, the number of successful tests, or other factors you have already discussed. In your presuppositions, you can also relate to time and number as required. Inoculations can use the same concepts, as should your presentation.

Criteria and Values in Presenting

You will have already elicited your customer's criteria and their values. You can and should use their criteria and values through out your sales presentation. The key to doing this is to note what they said were important to them and focus on the aspects of your product, service or offering that meets their criteria and to amplify them thoughout the sales call. These criteria and values need to have been consciously elicited in order to hold weight and they should also be expressed in the same influencing language that appeals to your customer. Values, as the driving force behind criteria, can be much more powerful as they can add extra strength to a truism or presupposition. Use their criteria and values throughout your presentation and do constantly use their own criteria to describe your product or service. This will make them feel like you have a much greater depth of understanding about their situation and this is what will make the presentation truly specific to them.

Making your Presenting More Compelling

Use stories, metaphors and anecdotes

Throughout our history this is the way we have learned and had our imagination fired, so using stories, metaphors and anecdotes is an incredibly powerful communication tool. You are forming images in your customer's mind, and images are far more potent than just words and will embed themselves more deeply into their consciousness. The advantage of stories and anecdotes is that they can really help you set the scene, they can also be great as part of your set-ups. Some people naturally use stories and anecdotes as part of their preferred style, whilst others may have to spend more time practicing to become comfortable with it. It's well worth spending the time to practice, as stories and images are naturally more interesting and captivating than plain information. They are also more memorable and longer lasting than words or instructions.

Use quotes

You can also tell a bit of a story by quoting what someone else has said. Quoting can take the heat off you or may even add credibility (depending on who the person you quote is) by landing full responsibility for what was said in the lap of that other person. It may allow you to say something you couldn't otherwise get away with yourself.

Angels and demons

For maximum impact, there are certain words you can add into your Set-Ups and Presentations that will get a positive response. These are your Angels.

Likewise, there are Demons that should be avoided at all costs. Some words are so negatively charged that they are best left out of any Set-Up or Presentation.

Angels

These words can do well wherever they are used. If they are hardwired in us, they will elicit a response and a positive state change. Angels can create impact, emphasis, anticipation and excitement. They are most effective when used in the right place with the right timing and intonation.

Commands

Start... Stop... Listen... Wait...

Any word or phrase that instructs someone to do something has a powerful and instant effect on us, whether we like it or not. This is language that puts you firmly in control. Commands are especially powerful when combined with 'now'. Commands are best given with a downward inflection to your tonality. An example might be…" **Now stop** for a moment and consider the long term benefits of our proposal…"

Descriptors

Amazingly, incredibly, significantly, easily, rapidly…

These adjective words and phrases can build excitement or underline what we are saying. They tend to catch our interest more than everyday information with no descriptors. As we have said Command language is distinguished by being spoken with a downturn in intonation at the end of the word or sentence. Descriptors should be used with more dramatic or enthusiastic intonation and careful timing to get maximum effect.

If you pepper your conversations with angels, your presentations will be much more powerful, compelling and memorable for your customer.

Demons

These are some words that are just inexcusable! Whilst some may be made to work for you if you control them properly, in general they are best avoided.

But

This is the chief demon and the one you will hear most often. Never, ever, use this in an answer to someone. As a response, it basically tells them you are going to ignore what they've just said to you. It is termed the 'universal negater', as it draws a line through the sentence said before it.

Hope (or Wish)

This simply smacks of despair. It looses credibility by indicating that you don't think it will happen but you'll hope and perhaps even pray anyway. And if that's how you feel, why would a customer trust you to deliver?!

Can't

This is a negative word. It indicates a lack of power or control on your part. Worse still, many people view it as a downright challenge—they'll want to see if they can! Best course of action is to avoid using it.

Try (or Attempt)

This can grate the way using 'Hope' does. Trying is not doing. If you promise to try to do something, to many people that's tantamount to saying you can't or won't.

These words are demons only in a sales or business context. There may be many times when you would use them socially for a number of reasons. For sales, find yourself some good alternatives and then practise avoiding your demons.

Take time to practice your presentations, especially the set-up, and the use of compelling language. The time you take to practice will more that pay off in the long run.

Chapter Six: Negotiations

Negotiating is probably the business skill that goes beyond all others. You will certainly need all the skills, knowledge and behaviours you have learned in previous chapters in order to negotiate successfully. Whatever business you are in, at some point in the transaction with your customer there is usually going to be some kind of negotiation. Something you want, something they want, some compromise, maybe something to be given up or something that can't be compromised. This is a critical stage in making your sale as you and your customer are at the point where you need to tie up all the loose ends before they are ready to make a commitment.

So, first things first, you need to establish which negotiating principle, and therefore which strategy, you feel is appropriate to each particular negotiation. This means your general approach, not your specific objectives. Your strategy determines how you intend to conduct the negotiation and the kind of effect it is likely to have. We need therefore to consider the spectrum of negotiation styles. These can broadly be considered as collaborative or competitive, in reality there are much finer distinctions to be made depending upon the degree to which you focus on your self and your own desired outcomes or how much you pay attention to others and what they want.

Focus on your own desired outcomes

This is a perfectly normal negotiation principle. The overall objective is to achieve something that you want. You will be drawn to your own outcomes. If you have no need to care about the other person's position or desired outcomes and therefore you are not interested in the relationship for the future then why not focus solely on your own desired outcome?

You do need to consider though that an exclusive focus on your own ends can be considered Machiavellian where the end justifies the means. This can lead to aggressive behaviour, intimidation or even deception in order to beat your opponent and to gain victory over them. This is a win—lose scenario with you as the winner.

Focus on the outcomes of others

Your ability to focus on others and their desired outcomes will depend very much on your values and beliefs about people. If you amplify the importance of others too highly then you will distort their importance in the transaction and prioritise their needs far beyond your own. This can easily happen if you have low self esteem for example.

Too much focus on the desired outcomes of others will necessitate the need for relentless concessions in the negotiation. This creates a lose–win scenario with you as the loser. Some people do like to play the role of the victim, but it is a very poor way in which to negotiate and it may well have a negative effect on the relationship as they may start to lose respect for you.

The middle ground between focusing on you focusing on them

In between the competition and the concession there is a balance that can be achieved. This area however may well be more variable than you might imagine. What may appear as a very collaborative negotiation may end up as more of a balance with some competitive elements. This is often achieved through the acknowledgement of each others criteria and use of shared values. This then creates a win—win scenario in which neither party feels to have been beaten.

The Process of Negotiation

When you have decided on the most appropriate strategy and style of negotiation that is best for your situation, you need to understand the process of negotiating. The act of negotiating can be broken down into separate chunks, which makes the process more manageable to explore. It's a logical progression that you can think of as what you do before the negotiation, what you do during the negotiation and what you do afterwards. Each chunk requires different skills, principles and techniques so we will look at them individually.

Negotiation Model and Related Skills

If you think of negotiation as a journey, then you have a clearly defined route to follow using this negotiation model as you move through the various stages to achieve a successful outcome. All the skills you require have already been outlined in previous chapters; you just need now to put them together in this order.

Planning and resources

This requires the skills that you have learned in previous chapters. This stage is all about state, goal clarity, and putting yourself in their shoes.

Determine outcome

This means determining both **your** outcome and **their** outcome. You do this by using questioning skills, criteria elicitation and once again putting yourself in their shoes.

Find area of common ground

The key elements of rapport with your customer—get goal clarity, put yourself in their shoes and establish rapport.

Control climate

Put yourself in charge of the conversation with verbal and nonverbal pacing and leading, and develop real communication with your customer.

Conclusion and agreement

The final stage where you need to keep focused. You use restating/backtracking, persuasion, gaining commitment.

Before the Negotiation

This part of the process consists of seven steps you want to have considered and have handled before the negotiation stage begins:

1. Prepare a resourceful state
2. Set outcomes
3. Consider concessions
4. Plan targeted questions
5. Set your evidence
6. Plan the venue
7. Plan tactics

What these individual steps do is crucial. They allow you to set the scene, determine the prevailing mood and influence and the effect the negotiation is likely to have on your relationship with the other person.

1. Prepare a Resourceful State

Before you even start planning a negotiation, get yourself into a resourceful state and answer the following question. What are your best states for planning a negotiation? Jot down your thoughts now.

During a negotiation you will find being able to access a variety of resourceful states essential. You will need to control the climate of the interaction. The climate or mood of the negotiation will be determined by how both parties behave. There will be times when you might need to be empathetic, times when you need to be curious, times when you need to be confident, strong or assertive. Now you need to brainstorm what states you might need for various parts of the negotiation. Ensure you can trigger the state you want when you come to negotiate. Also give some thought to the kind of state that will be useful to elicit in your customer. What states do you want your customer in? You might find that your client is in a state that is not going to be conducive for you to have a successful negotiation, in which case you will need to be prepared to change their state. You already know the secret to changing someone else's state—go there first.

2. Determine your Outcomes: What do you want?

The next step in your preparation is to identify what you really want out of this negotiation. This seems obvious I know, but some people who find themselves negotiating don't understand their own criteria let alone their goals for the negotiation.

Set your priorities

Differentiate between your criteria—which modal operators are you attaching to your list of criteria. Which are a necessity and therefore essential and which are a possibility and therefore nice to have. In short work out what is more important to you and what is less important.

Common areas of importance are time and money. Are these important to you in the negotiation you are planning? Do you need a settlement now or are you prepared to let proceedings go on for a little while. Is the financial situation vital for you or can you be flexible enough to ensure a good deal on other aspects of the negotiation? As ever the more flexible you can be the better the chances are of achieving a successful and satisfying outcome.

Set your boundaries

It is not enough to just know what you want in a negotiation you have to understand what your Best Possible Outcome (BPO) is and what is your Worst Acceptable Position

(WAP). Once you have determined these what will be your opening position? Too high and you could offend or even frighten them off. Too low and you could lose out. Your opening offer should be based on a number of things, the value of the things you want, the situation the other person is in and the climate you want to create within the negotiation. In reality you will be able to reassess your opening position especially if the other party makes their opening offer first, however it is still a very valuable exercise to plan your opening position.

By setting the outcome, you are establishing your control over the situation from the start. These are the key questions you need to consider.

The bargaining arena

As part of the planning stage, you need to judge if there is any likely overlap between your outcomes and theirs for each issue. If there is an overlap, then there should be a Realistic Settlement Point somewhere between your BPO and your WAP and their WAP and their BPO. It is this overlap that is your bargaining arena and if there is no overlap, then no settlement is possible.

Crucial steps to setting your outcomes

i) **Use your imagination** to list all the objectives you could possibly want to achieve in the negotiation, from the most mundane to the most incredibly idealistic. Go prepared with a shopping list. Remember aim high!

ii) **Prioritise** by deciding whether you most want to achieve the short-term or long-term objectives on the list.

iii) **Reality check**: eliminate the goals you feel cannot possibly be achieved. However, you want to aim to retain that state of creative optimism for the actual negotiation.

iv) **Put yourself in their shoes** and repeat the previous three steps. You want to identify likely conflicts between your goals and their probable goals so that you can prepare ways to resolve them. *(Refer back to Chapter 1: Personal Success Strategies to remind you).*

v) **Keep your outcomes in mind** throughout the entire negotiation. Make sure you examine everything that happens in terms of how it affects your outcomes.

3. Consider Concessions

The third part of our seven stage negotiation planning process is considering the necessity of making certain concessions in order to gain the outcomes you need. So you need to consider what concessions you might trade. There is just one golden rule for planning concessions: **Only plan to concede issues that are perceived as high value to the other side, but that are in fact low value to you.**

When you are planning what concessions you could make you need to follow a simple process every time. First identify the issue before you value the £ cost to your organisation and whether that is a one-off or ongoing cost. Next consider what monetary or other value that concession is worth to the other party and then link it to another issue. Having done all that, you would then consider what are the issues you can trade with the customer?

The value of concessions:

Bear in mind that the value of a concession is defined by the benefit the *receiver* gets, not what it is worth to you. Put yourself in their shoes and use the following **SPACED** guide to determine what the benefits to them (and therefore likely value) will be.

These are only types of benefit a concession can provide:

Security:	Safety, lack of risk, confidence, peace of mind
Performance:	Doing the job quicker, better, up to standard
Appearance:	Looking good or organisation looking good
Convenience:	Life made easier, less hassle
Economy:	Money, lump sum, payment terms, profit, value
Durability:	Lasting, enduring service or relationship

As you plan your list of potential concessions check them against the SPACED criteria. This way, you can easily emphasise these benefits to the other person when you come to make the concession.

4. Plan your Questions

As in any other field, the more you do your homework, the better the result will be. If you are used to working 'off the cuff' this may seem unnecessary to you, but by planning the questions ahead of time you have more control over the whole process and are more likely to get the information you need during the negotiation. The key areas that you want to include are: eliciting their criteria and values *(Refer back to Chapter 4: Criteria Elicitation)*, identifying their outcomes (BPO/WAP), and providing information that will help you to assess the value (to them) of a concession.

Again, the most useful skill when planning these is Putting Yourself in Their Shoes. *(Refer back to Chapter 1: Personal Success Strategies)*. This will enable you to phrase your questions in an appealing as well as targeted way, to get you what you need to know. Remember you can also employ techniques such as using Softeners to help to build rapport and doing so may give you permission to ask the more awkward or sensitive questions. *(Chapter 4: Criteria Elicitation)*

5. Set the Evidence

How will you know the negotiation is going your way? You need evidence, so part of the planning process is to brainstorm ideas as to what success signs you need to look for during the negotiation. The best evidence is sensory evidence; future pace the negotiation, what I mean by this is it plays through in your mind like a movie. See yourself achieving just what you want and notice how you will feel when you achieve it. Notice what you will be seeing and hearing.

6. Plan the Venue: Home or Away?

You may not always have a choice, but it is important because where you meet for a negotiation makes quite a difference to its climate. There are benefits to having it at home

… or away and meeting on 'neutral' territory, like a hotel, is an option, provided it's genuinely neutral to both parties. Having the meeting on your own home ground has many advantages. You will probably feel more in control and you can orchestrate recesses and breaks to suit you. It is up to you to choose the layout of the meeting to suit you and you have control over whether there are any interruptions. You can also gain a moral advantage if they're late, and you have access to support being available on site to break any deadlocks

The advantages to having the meeting away are not so many, but can be just as useful to you. For instance it gives you an opportunity to assess the other party's workplace and they may make allowances to you as you are not on home ground. It is also possible you can pressurise the other party by suggesting that senior staff also get involved in the negotiation.

7. Plan Tactics

Finally, you are ready to plan your tactics, and these are the actions you take during the negotiation to implement your strategy. You might include here setting the prevailing mood for the negotiation and presenting material evidence to support your case, such as references or statistics. Your tactics will certainly include planning what concessions you are prepared to make during the negotiation and can include behaviours which could force the other party to make a concession.

Restraint

You can adopt this tactic—that is doing nothing—when the other party is expecting a reaction from you. If you feel that they are trying to provoke you in some way then just do nothing and wait for their next action. This is a non-confrontational way of showing that that you will not be swayed and are sticking to your position.

Piece by piece

The principle behind this tactic is that if you want someone to give you something large that they may be reluctant to consider, then it's better to ask for it a piece at a time in a way they feel they can cope with rather than demand the whole thing in one go.

Artificial deadline

If you wish to pressurise the other party into a quick deal, then you can set an artificial deadline to force them into a decision. This is a very frequently used method in consumer selling such as 'sale price only available until 5pm today'.

Over their head

If the negotiation reaches a deadlock situation that you are unable to resolve in any other way, then one tactic can be to ask to deal with a superior instead. This really is only to be used as a last resort as doing so will almost certainly alienate the original negotiating team.

During the Negotiation

There are several things to do once the negotiation starts:

1. Maintain state and rapport

2. Chunk the negotiation
3. Handle concessions
4. Seek congruent agreement
5. Summarise & Backtrack

Despite having many things you may need to discuss in a negotiation, don't forget there is one very powerful technique you can apply at any time—**SILENCE.** You do not need to keep talking, or fill every gap in the conversation. If you have asked for a concession and don't get an immediate response, don't try to justify it and rush in with more reasons or options, just wait. The pressure of silence can be incredibly potent. If you are patient the other party usually feels the need to respond and fill that gap.

1. Maintain State and Rapport

Beware of the prevailing mood because it can be infectious, that's why it's important that you create the mood first where you can. If you are getting a negative mood produced by the client, then remember there is always a positive response that will counter it. So if you feel the mood getting away from you, you can do something about it and change it to be effective for your purposes. These are some examples of what you might encounter, and what you want to produce to change it:

Negative Climate:	**Positive Climate:**
Agitated	Calming
Apathetic	Dynamic
Defensive	Supportive

Dogmatic	Creative
Hostile	Helpful
Prejudiced	Open-minded
Suspicious	Open
Thoughtless	Considerate
Unprincipled	Ethical

Once again it is vitally important that you keep putting yourself in their shoes throughout the negotiation. If you are fully focused on this, then if the situation turns negative it can help you understand why it is happening. Once you have that information you are in a much better position to work out how to adjust your style to improve the atmosphere. The more you learn about the other person through the negotiation, the more you will be able to refine your negotiating techniques and this will lead you to much better outcomes.

2. Chunk the Negotiation

It usually helps to break a negotiation into chunks and this is done in two ways: chunking up and chunking down. You want to start the negotiation by determining all the areas of common agreement, what you both agree on and hold in common. Once that is established then you can move on.

'Chunking up':

This means talking about issues on a more general level. You will do this by pacing their reality and making statements of irrefutable truth. For instance 'We are meeting today because you have asked me to look at how you can improve your sales on this specific range' of course you must only state what is true and not up for any question or dispute between you. This leads to a building of rapport, gains agreement and starts to build trust. This is the perfect place to use a Set-up as we discussed in the chapter about presenting.

After this general 'chunking up', you are ready to start addressing the issues with them. One reason negotiations can go wrong is because the two parties start the communication with the main issue. This is where the emotion is. So it is far better to chunk up to the highest level of agreement.

'Chunking down':

Think about the specific issues raised and chunk down to these. Make sure each issue is chunked down individually, not lumped together. This not only makes them more manageable but it also allows you to focus deeply on just one issue at a time.

3. Handle Concessions

Whatever your reason for offering concessions, and no matter how easy or unimportant you think the concession is to you, you must follow the golden rule.

Always make sure you get something in return

If you are not certain about how to make concessions work for you, there are a number of useful guidelines for you to follow:

- Always present a concession as 'I will'...then 'you can/will...'
- Allow room to negotiate a concession
- Encourage them to reveal their demands first
- Make your concession first
- Make them work for each concession
- Give concessions that give 'nothing' away
- Remember, even saying 'I'll consider it' is a concession
- Don't be afraid to say 'no'
- Keep a tally of your concessions (and theirs) so that you can refer back to them, when backtracking
- Don't give too much or too quickly
- Don't be afraid to retreat from a concession if you've made a mistake

4. Seek Congruent Agreement

Any proposed solution has to work for both parties and be acceptable to them. This is essential if you want to have a long-lasting agreement and continuing good relationships with them as your outcome. Both sides need to clearly demonstrate through both words and actions that they are in agreement with the outcome. You can check this by seeing if they are walking their talk and appear to be in rapport with themselves. If they do have an internal conflict around the agreement they may show it for example by agreeing verbally so the words sound right, but they may use a doubtful or hesitant tonality or adopt an uncomfortable body posture. So you have a frame of reference for this, think about when people have been incongruent with you in meetings or conversation. What have you noticed about their words, tonality, posture, or demeanour?

5. Summarise & Backtrack

Frequent backtracking allows everyone to keep track of and agree the negotiation's progress, which helps to avoid surprise misunderstandings.

For this reason, paraphrasing should be avoided when doing this. It tends to lead to more misunderstandings. Instead, Parrot Phrase the key points using their own words, and mirroring their tone of voice and body language. This pacing helps both to maintain rapport and reassure the other person that they have been fully understood. It also keeps the negotiation moving towards agreement. You can also summarise the key negotiation points by using the phrase 'So if...' and then listing them as you have so far agreed. This can be a great way of doing a trial close to see if you are near to a commitment.

There are some key words and phrases to use when you are backtracking and summarising and the most powerful language uses words that demonstrate the other person's criteria and values. You can emphasise these using tonality and gestures but please, please don't assume you know exactly what these words mean to the other person, just parrot phrase them back without any comment or addition

After the Negotiation

After the negotiation it is essential for you to keep the process together.

One the deal has been struck and an acceptable agreement to both parties has been reached, that's the first step. You now have to track the negotiation following the agreed tracking methods. You must deliver what you promised, and ensure that your counterpart does the same. If it is genuinely viewed as a win-win situation why not celebrate your success with a joint lunch or dinner. You may even want to send them a token thank-you gift to reinforce the relationship and invoke the rule of reciprocity (Refer to next chapter)

Follow up within at least two days of the negotiation to check for any outstanding issues and deal with these immediately. This part of the process really is just about common courtesy and integrity. Be responsible and stick to your end of the bargain by completing your tasks on time and in full. In other words don't leave any loose ends that could trip you up later.

Once again it can be very useful to mentally rehearse the agreement by future pacing it. Use the power of your imagination to visualise how it is going to work out. Imagine what might go wrong and think about how you can fix this within the terms of the agreement.

I am sure you know by now that the secret to successful negotiation is in the planning and preparation that you do before the actual negotiation takes place.

This really is a case of failure to plan is planning to fail.

Chapter Seven: Gaining Commitment

We talked at the beginning at the book about giving you a route map, and we have progressed through the various places you needed to visit before the destination was in sight. We set off with your Personal Success Strategies, developed your Relationship Building and Behaviour Profiling techniques, then discovered how to successfully elicit the client's criteria, improved your presentation and lastly mastered the art of negotiation.

Now, we are ready for the last element, because gaining commitment from your customer is the final stage of your journey. First let's clear up any misunderstandings about what I mean by 'gaining commitment'. It is NOT about using 'closing techniques'. In fact it is more about opening than closing. There is an awful lot of rubbish written and indeed spoken about closing in a sales context. The ABC or always be closing school of selling is a very crass approach to a process that can be so very elegant. However cleverly you manage your closing, it will not work unless you have successfully convinced your customer they will *benefit* from taking action.

Gaining commitment IS all about working towards your end point right from the start. To do this effectively, it helps to understand why the techniques in this book are so powerful in a sales situation. There are fundamental principles (or rules) of the human psyche that seem to be present when people are influenced and drive our behaviour very strongly. Much of this work was done by a psychologist named Dr Robert Cialdini and was published in his book 'The science of influence'. There are 7 rules that govern everyone and these are consistency, authority, reciprocity, contrast, association/liking, scarcity and social proof. Once you have understood them, they can be leveraged in a number of ways.

1. The Rule of Consistency

Once we have expressed an opinion about, or taken a stand on, a particular issue, we tend to strongly defend our statement—regardless of its accuracy.

How it works

Consistency is viewed as a positive trait because it equates to stability and sanity. So it seems we all want to be (or appear) consistent with our attitudes, beliefs and actions. Interestingly, the consistency rule holds true even when our initial belief or statement is shown to be wildly inaccurate. So saying, writing or doing something creates a strong urge in someone to make their future behaviour consistent with that. Thus, it encourages commitment and **the more public the statement or action, the more potent its effect.** Remember that verbal statements have considerable impact, but written statements are the most effective and the more people who witness any statement, the better.

How to leverage it

Once we have said or done something, it becomes very hard to back down without appearing inconsistent. That's why encouraging someone to state their criteria means they are more likely to stick to them in future. The successful professional Sales person will use the rule of consistency in subtle yet powerful ways. They will elicit the client's criteria and values, by asking "what is important to them about...?" And finding out their values by asking "what does that (Their Criteria) do for you?" Then they will use their criteria and values as leverage when presenting what their offering will do for them.

Sales professional: "What is important to you about the new computer system you are going to buy?"

Customer: "It needs to cut our running costs whilst increasing our profitability"

If the sales professional can demonstrate that their product or service can reduce running costs and increase profitability, it is unlikely that the customer will turn around and say that those elements are not important to them.

The best of the best therefore would use the rule of consistency in virtually all of their sales presentations.

The consistency rule is one great way to gain commitment and therefore compliance.

One small action or statement can kick off commitment to a consistent course of action. This gives you the chance to follow this through and generate bigger and bigger commitments in future.

2. The Rule of Authority

When we are unsure what action to take, we tend to defer to people whom we perceive are in a position of authority or power.

How it works

Our brains are constantly looking for shortcuts that allow us to spend less time making decisions. A useful shortcut that usually works is to follow people with superior wisdom, skill or experience and, in general, these people tend to be those in higher positions of authority than us. Provided the authority they wield is legitimate, it is a useful rule to follow. Authority seems to be created by the following equation.

Authority = Expertise + Trustworthiness

How to leverage it

Ideally, you want to reach a position of natural authority with your customers, so we need to look at expertise and trustworthiness in relation to that.

Expertise can be established through casual conversation with your customers, as this is a great way in which you can reveal your level of expertise and has the added bonus of being relatively quick. Credibility, or authority, is also communicated through congruent confidence (but not conceit or arrogance) and, don't forget that rapport also plays a crucial role in your customer's perception of your credibility. Carefully crafted stories of your experiences with similar clients in similar circumstances can help you gain credibility with your customers. They will see this as evidence that you are in a position to help them with their decision.

Trust is vitally important component of authority, and often takes considerable time to establish. A key element of trust involves being seen as unbiased, so if you are confident enough to demonstrate a shortcoming of your offering before moving on to the benefits, this can help give your customer the perception of your being unbiased and therefore trustworthy.

Recently when I went to buy a car from a local dealership, the salesman used the rules of Consistency and Authority together with great effect. I had done all my research and was fairly sure that I wanted the model I had chosen, I just needed a test drive before making my mind up. When the salesman approached me I explained my situation and that I just needed to drive the car. However I was surprised that the process was not going to be so simple. The salesman actually said that before we go for a drive he needed to speak with me about the car, because as he put it "This model is not for everyone". Thus proving to me he was not just going to sell me the car for the sake of it—he needed to know that the car and I were compatible. When we sat down he asked me what was important to me about the car I was about to buy. He elicited all my criteria and then said "well it certainly seems like this is the car for you". Then when we were on the test drive he just kept pointing out how this particular model met my criteria perfectly.

3. The Rule of Reciprocity

Being given something of perceived value creates a strong desire in us to give something back in return.

How it works

Reciprocity is instilled in us from a very young age. You get to play with young George's truck if you let him play with your fire engine, and so on. It applies a degree of 'fairness' to social interactions and without it, it would be difficult for society to function as it does. People who take but don't give back are generally frowned upon. So we are conditioned to give gifts or favours in return for receiving them. Amazingly, you don't have to ask for the gift to feel you should give something in return because even an unsolicited gift still fosters a feeling of obligation.

Perhaps more surprisingly, we don't even have to want the gift for the feelings of reciprocity to kick in. But a desirable gift creates a stronger response. More incredibly still, what you do in return for the gift does not have to be equal in size or value. However we feel life is fairest when they are roughly equivalent. Rewards don't work the same way. It's being the first to give that puts you in a powerful position within the relationship.

How to leverage it

You could simply decide what you want from someone, give them an unsolicited/unwanted gift and try to get what you want back. But when using this cold-blooded approach, the rule does not work as effectively as it could.

The higher the gift's perceived value, or its desirability, the stronger the feeling of reciprocity and the more satisfied your customer will be with the transaction. Giving something to your customer can be a very powerful compliance driver which is why giving samples and other free gifts is so popular, and generally effective. This is a technique used very effectively by supermarkets, cosmetics companies and pharmaceutical companies all of which use samples as a way increasing compliance.

In negotiation, being the first to give a valuable concession can be a powerful gesture and can invoke the rule of reciprocity. This may mean your proposal is not rejected, and lead them to offer a concession of high value to you in return.

Don't be too narrow minded here, gifts don't have to be objects, in fact some of the less tangible offerings can be the most powerful, these can include information, cooperation, listening, time, friendship or trust.

4. The Rule of Contrast

When two slightly different things are presented one immediately after the other, the second one will seem more different than it really is.

Why it works

Our minds are constantly comparing the similarities and differences between things around us. When we see two slightly different things together, our brains tend to exaggerate the differences between them. If we lift a heavy object followed by a lighter one, the latter seems lighter to us than it would have if it had been the only one we'd lifted.

How to leverage it

By putting two products or services together in the mind of your customer, you will encourage them to focus more on which to buy, rather than whether to buy at all. The rule of contrast makes people think about differences, and differences encourage us in turn to think about our preferences. Show the choice you'd like your customer to take, or the least expensive option, to them last. If they feel compelled to buy something, the cheapest option will seem like pocket money by comparison. Contrast also means that selling accessories and add-ons is much easier immediately after a major purchase. This is because the price of the extras seems so tiny in contrast to the large investment.

You might not normally spend £100 on a shirt, however the salesman in the designer clothes shop knows that after you have spent £495 on a new designer suit, it will much easier to sell you a relatively expensive shirt and tie. In contrast to the price of the suit at that moment in time the shirt appears quite inexpensive.

After spending hundreds of pounds on a new television the £35.95 the electrical shop is asking for the extended warranty seems cheap. I heard a story of a salesman who was targeted to sell extended warranties with his top-end audio systems. He understood the principles of the rule of contrast and used it to great effect. The shop offered different levels of extended warranty cover. The top end warranty was extremely expensive. He found that if he offered the most expensive cover first, he would get rejection from the customer. He could then offer one of the cheaper policies and the customer would gratefully accept his proposal as it now appeared relatively inexpensive. He didn't care which policy they bought, he was only targeted on the number of extended warranties he sold, not which ones.

Presenting the cheapest option first will make the thing you present second seem even more expensive. This will probably not serve many sale situations very well at all.

Here is an example of a young student's use of the perceptual contrast principle.

Dear Mum and Dad

I am sorry I have not written for sometime. I know I should have written more frequently, but I thought I would write and bring you up to date with how things are going here at university. Before you read on please sit down. You do need to be sat down and prepared to hear my news.

I am getting along quite nicely now. The fractured skull I received when I jumped out of my window when my flat caught fire is just about healed. I only had to spend a couple of weeks in the ICU unit and I can honestly say that the double vision has past and the headaches are far less frequent now. I was very lucky really. The guy that called the fire brigade when he saw my flat on fire visited me in hospital. When he realised I now had nowhere to live he invited me to stay with him. His place is not in a very nice area of town, I have to admit, but he is quite cute and we have fallen madly in love with each other. We plan to marry before my pregnancy starts to show.

Yes, I am pregnant and I am sure you are really looking forward to becoming grandparents. I am sure you will be very proud of your first grand child and give him (or her) the same deep love and affection you have always given me. Although my new love has a criminal record and had only just come out of prison the day before the fire, I am sure you will welcome him in to our family with open arms.

Now that you are up to date with recent events, I have to tell you that there was no fire and therefore I did not jump from the window and fracture my skull. No I was not in ICU for two weeks and I am certainly not pregnant and there is no dodgy boy friend. I have however failed my first year at University and I have to re-sit the whole year. I just wanted you to see this in perspective!

5. The Rule of Liking

We like people who we feel are similar to us, and we also like those people who like us and are prepared to say so.

How it works

There are three key components that cause people to like each other:

Similarity: where we have, or perceive we have, shared attitudes, backgrounds, and experiences
Praise: we tend to believe praise and to like those who provide it
Cooperation: when we are working towards common goals with someone it makes us like each other more

It is human nature to actively seek similarities between us and those we come in contact with. It is these similarities that enable us to associate with a group that we feel good about. Advertisers are very well aware of this, and it is why they seek celebrity endorsements. When we use the same product as a celebrity we admire it makes us feel more closely associated with them as a result. The rule of liking is why the process of building rapport involves matching and pacing on many levels because it increases the perceived similarity between two people. We all want to feel good about ourselves and it is human nature to respond positively to praise, provided it is given sincerely. You must find something genuine to give praise for, as everyone can see through false compliments because they are so transparently untrue and usually fail in their attempts to influence. Even if people think they are totally different from each other in many ways, by working together to achieve a common aim it makes them more likely to feel favourably towards one another.

How to leverage it

85% of the decision making process comes down to what you feel about the person who is trying to sell to you. Relationship in other words, and really effective persuaders take the time to get to know their clients, and therefore make it more likely that similarities (or perceived similarities) will be discovered. The key to successfully leveraging the rule of liking lies once again in finding <u>genuine</u> ways to like someone else. By acting congruently you are not only true to yourself, but avoid the disastrous situation of being seen as slimy or insincere neither of which is a trustworthy state. Once you have established a good relationship with your customer, it can be powerful to let them know you like them or like working with them—whatever is most appropriate for your style and the context you work in.

Cooperation or working together to solve a common problem

is a powerful team-building tool. When working with people in this way it seems to have the effect of building robust relationships that can last and endure and this can help achieve compliance with in that team.

6. The Rule of Scarcity

When something we want appears rare or restricted, we tend to want it more and place a higher value on it than if it were freely available.

How it works

People naturally find items that are scarce, or getting scarcer, more attractive. This tendency appears to stem from a basic need to compete for limited resources, but the rule applies to everything, even non-essential items like gems or precious metals, which have a great perceived value. It is human nature to ignore something or take it for granted, only to suddenly desire it when it is no longer available or about to be taken away. This can be seen in any locality where a resource such as a library or a theatre is about to close for lack of support, on hearing of the closure suddenly people don't want to lose the facility and start using it again, even if only for a limited time.

How to leverage it

Make your customer aware that something about you, your product or your services is scarce: the time you have, the quantity available, the duration of a promotion. 'This offer is only available until midnight tonight!' is one internet sales gambit that is frequently used and can be copied in many other areas where it's appropriate. You also need to highlight the ways in which your offering is unique or rare for example such as 'the only vacuum cleaner that is self-emptying' or 'Just 100 of these cars were ever manufactured and this is one of only three left in the world' because this will help to encourage customers to place a higher value on them. Competition amplifies the scarcity effect, so if you demonstrate that competition exists, you can increase the demand for something.

A client of mine uses a combination of the rule of reciprocity and the rule of scarcity with her customers all the time. She likes to provide excellent customer service and one way she does this is by telephoning her customers and giving them hot off the press industry information, for which they are eternally grateful. This combination works well for my client and increases compliance with her customers.

7. The Rule of Social Proof

When deciding if we should do something, we tend to take the lead from similar people in a similar situation so we can judge if a given behaviour is acceptable.

How it works

Wanting to feel accepted is a natural human urge, we want to belong and be part of the group. We often wonder 'what will people think?' whether we are aware of it consciously or not. When making a decision we may be subconsciously hoping for the approval of others, and will therefore look around to see what behaviour is likely to bring approval. It's also possible that we may be genuinely confused about what to do in a situation, and therefore mimicking the behaviour of others can seem like a shortcut to making a good decision. In general, the rule of social proof helps us to make quick and efficient decisions that are usually correct. The power of social proof is amplified when certain conditions are present:

- greater numbers of people doing the same thing
- if we perceive them to be very similar to us and in a similar situation to us
- if we feel uncertain about what action to take and how to proceed

How to leverage it

At some level it is important to assure your customer that buying your product or service is a fantastic idea. Demonstrating that others have made a similar decision and had successful outcomes is an elegant way to invoke the rule of social proof. The more people in a similar position who have made the same decision, the better! And the more uncertain your customer, the more likely they will look to social proof for a possible answer.

Many pharmaceutical companies use a combination of the rule of authority and the rule of social proof by using Key opinion leaders, often eminent clinicians in their field, to provide what is supposed to appear as impartial evidence of the efficacy of their drugs. The knowledge that leaders in their field is using and champions a product is important to a decision maker. It is certainly incredibly effective to have testimonials from satisfied customers, providing evidence that other people have bought your product or service and are satisfied.

We have now reached the end of your journey to achieving the professional edge in selling. Many of the secrets, strategies and techniques I have shared with you will help you move from hoping and praying you have got it right, to knowing you are taking the luck out of selling by using the science of excellence. Do keep returning to the book and practicing until you have got the structure of your sales technique flowing naturally and easily, and as ever, the more you practice the better, and the luckier, you will get.

Take the luck out of selling
—*use* the secrets of the science of excellence!

Acknowledgements

I have seen many of the ideas in this book presented in a variety of different ways, the secret to these particular strategies presented in Taking the luck out of selling…, is that they work. I know this from seeing the effects many times over on sales professionals who are willing to step out of their comfort zone and try new approaches to selling and influence & persuasion.

A big part of my journey of discovery has been finding the originators of the work that has had such a profound effect on my effectiveness, and working and training with them.

I have been very fortunate to have studied with some of the best trainers of NLP in the world. In addition to Richard Bandler these include Paul McKenna, Michael Breen, John LaValle, Shelle Rose Charvet and Eric Robbie. I need to thank these people for contributing to my own personal success in business, as a consultant and trainer. I apologise if there are any people I have missed out.

ISBN 142512204-3

Printed in Great Britain
by Amazon